INNOVATING FOR THE GLOBAL SOUTH
Towards an Inclusive Innovation Agenda

Edited by Dilip Soman, Janice Gross Stein, and Joseph Wong

Despite the vast wealth generated globally in the last half-century, inequality is worsening and poverty is becoming increasingly chronic throughout much of the southern hemisphere. Hundreds of millions of people continue to live on less than $2 per day and lack basic human necessities such as nutritious food, shelter, clean water, primary health care, and education.

Innovating for the Global South offers fresh solutions for reducing poverty in the developing world, highlighting the multidisciplinary expertise of the University of Toronto's Global Innovation Group. In this collection of original essays, leading experts from the fields of engineering, medicine, management, and global public policy examine the causes and consequences of endemic poverty and the challenges of mitigating its effects from the perspective of the world's poorest of the poor.

Can we imagine ways to generate solar energy to run essential medical equipment in the countryside? Can we adapt information and communication technologies to provide up-to-the-minute agricultural market prices for remote farming villages? How do we create innovation processes that are inclusive and respond to the needs of those living in urban slums? Is it possible to invent a low-cost toilet that operates beyond the water and electricity grids?

Dedicated to the goal of stimulating, delivering, and harnessing innovation in the developing world, *Innovating for the Global South* is essential reading for managers, practitioners, and scholars in the areas of development, business, and policy.

DILIP SOMAN is Corus Chair in Communication Strategy and a Professor of Marketing at the Rotman School of Management, University of Toronto.

JANICE GROSS STEIN is the Belzberg Professor of Conflict Management in the Department of Political Science and Director of the Munk School of Global Affairs at the University of Toronto.

JOSEPH WONG is Ralph and Roz Halbert Professor of Innovation at the Munk School of Global Affairs and Canada Research Chair in Democratization, Health, and Development in the Department of Political Science at the University of Toronto.

The Munk Series on Global Affairs

This series of agenda-setting books aims to confront and explain big ideas critical to contemporary global affairs – from global innovation, security, and justice, to the global economy – in a brief, accessible format. Each expert author in the Munk Series roster employs rich examples to tell a powerful global story and inform a broad audience with an interest in current affairs.

EDITED BY DILIP SOMAN, JANICE GROSS STEIN,
AND JOSEPH WONG

Innovating for
the Global South

Towards an Inclusive Innovation
Agenda

UNIVERSITY OF TORONTO PRESS
Toronto Buffalo London

© University of Toronto Press 2014
Rotman–UTP Publishing
University of Toronto Press
Toronto Buffalo London
www.utppublishing.com
Printed in Canada

ISBN 978-1-4426-4676-6 (cloth)
ISBN 978-1-4426-1462-8 (paper)

Printed on acid-free, 100% post-consumer recycled paper with vegetable-based inks

Library and Archives Canada Cataloguing in Publication

Innovating for the global south: towards an inclusive innovation agenda
edited by Dilip Soman, Janice Gross Stein, and Joseph Wong.

Includes bibliographical references.
ISBN 978-1-4426-4676-6 (bound).   ISBN 978-1-4426-1462-8 (pbk.)

1. Technological innovations – Developing countries.   2. Technological
innovations – Social aspects – Developing countries.   I. Soman, Dilip, editor
of compilation   II. Stein, Janice, editor of compilation   III. Wong, Joseph,
1973–, editor of compilation

HC59.72.T4155 2014   338'.064091724   C2013-906837-6

University of Toronto Press acknowledges the financial assistance to its
publishing program of the Canada Council for the Arts and the Ontario Arts
Council.

Canada Council   Conseil des Arts
for the Arts   du Canada

ONTARIO ARTS COUNCIL
CONSEIL DES ARTS DE L'ONTARIO
50 YEARS OF ONTARIO GOVERNMENT SUPPORT OF THE ARTS
50 ANS DE SOUTIEN DU GOUVERNEMENT DE L'ONTARIO AUX ARTS

University of Toronto Press acknowledges the financial support of the
Government of Canada through the Canada Book Fund for its publishing
activities.

Contents

INNOVATING FOR THE GLOBAL SOUTH

Towards an Inclusive Innovation Agenda

Introduction
Rethinking Innovation

JOSEPH WONG

DILIP SOMAN

Basic sanitation, access to clean water, and hygiene are all things that *many* of us living in the First World take for granted. Consider, however, that according to United Nations (UN) estimates, nearly 2.5 billion people, or about 40 per cent of the world's population, do not have access to basic sanitation and clean drinking water. Access to sanitation is a global challenge, and the implications of such limited access are manifold, particularly for those who are very poor. We know, for instance, that infant mortality rates in the developing world can be drastically reduced and child development enhanced if children have access to basic sanitation. We also know that more than 2 million people die each year because of diarrheal disease, which is connected to poor sanitation. Humans suffer, and productivity suffers as well. Estimates show that economic output equivalent to over 5 billion productive days (working days) is lost each year because of diarrhea-related disease; the lack of proper sanitation constrains economic development. The images of open defecation, flooded pit latrines, and contaminated water remind one of the images of Dickensian London. The tragedy, of course, is that Dickens's England is of the nineteenth century. According to a recent survey conducted by the *British Medical Journal*, the "provision of clean water and sewage disposal" was found to have had the greatest medical and health impact in the last century and a half. And yet nearly half of the world's population continue to lack this basic amenity. Dickens's London has changed, but tragically, for many in the developing world – the Global South – such conditions persist.

The UN's Millennium Development Goals (MDGs), established in 2000, were intended to address the many challenges adversely affecting the world's poor, including broadening access to basic sanitation. Building upon a human-centred development agenda, the MDGs address myriad challenges, from poverty to maternal and child health to female empowerment to environmental sustainability. The MDGs have accomplished many things. They have facilitated greater Global North and South collaboration in the area of human development, reoriented and thus broadened development goals, and reshaped the relationship between the public and private sectors, fundamentally altering prevailing conceptions of how states and markets interact. Most important, the MDGs, as a coherent, exhaustive, and mutually reinforcing set of development objectives, drew tremendous attention to important global challenges and issues engaging governments, business, and citizen activists – key stakeholders who had until recently viewed these basic development objectives as the responsibility of those in the Global South, or the "Third World." Lack of social, economic, and sustainable development – or underdevelopment – was *their* problem.

Since then, Bill Gates has made a global impact more through his development work with the Bill and Melinda Gates Foundation than through Microsoft; scholarly tracts that lay out the policy and business implications of behavioural economics and experimental work on randomized control trials (such as Banerjee's and Duflo's *Poor Economics)* have become bestsellers; academic pundits such as William Easterly and Jeffrey Sachs are fuelling heated debates about consumer behaviour among the poorest of the poor; development assistance programs and government-funded foreign aid schemes are increasingly working with private sector actors; civil society organizations and critical scholars (such as the United Kingdom's Guy Standing) are making a pitch for innovative *unconditional* cash transfer (or basic income) programs; and profit-making firms and venture capitalists are thinking seriously about corporate social responsibility, impact investing, and the double bottom line. These exciting developments are a consequence, both directly and indirectly, of the agenda-setting effect of the work of the United Nations in establishing specific development goals to be achieved by 2015.

The MDGs, and the timeline attached to them, stimulated new investments, both public and private, in development in the Global South. Yet in some respects, to the extent that the MDGs have been reached, it appears they are being reached because we are *collectively doing more* by spending more, providing more, and paying more attention. Notwithstanding some key innovations in development – many of which are discussed in this book – one could argue, however, that we have been *doing more of the same* and with greater conviction. Doing more has laudably mitigated the effects of some of these basic human and development challenges, but it is the "more" that is doing the bulk of the work. After all, the MDG for sanitation specifically aims to reduce by 50 per cent the number of people without access to basic sanitation by 2015, though it does not look as though that target will be reached. Could we be doing more to approach that MDG and, indeed, the new MDGs that will soon be announced? Yes. But could we be doing things more innovatively, efficiently, effectively, sensibly, and with greater contextual sensitivity? Absolutely. The point is that while "doing more, spending more, and paying more attention" to issues related to development are obviously important, *doing things better and with greater and more efficient impact*, it seems to us, is even more important. The post-2015 world requires new strategies and approaches to development and poverty reduction. This is where innovation comes in.

Innovating for the Global South

Innovation is a ubiquitous term; everyone wants to get into the innovation game. This makes sense. With the global economy moving farther from Fordist models of manufacturing – of making things – and with over-reliance on commodities appearing to be an uncertain economic strategy for the long-term, more and more people are looking to leverage their knowledge and to use human knowledge capital to drive their innovation economies. But innovation, we know, is a high-stakes game. Failures abound.

Innovation demands enormous sunk investments. Commercially successful innovations are rare and tend to be priced very high in the market, as innovators seek to recoup their investments through price inflation rather than volume. Product innovators such as Apple, Google, GE, and "big pharma" effectively exploit the logic of supply-induced demand among those who can pay: "I don't need an iPad but I want one and I can afford one." Thus, for many critical scholars and on-the-ground practitioners of development, particularly those working with and in the Global South, innovation and innovation studies are not particularly helpful; in fact, the distributive consequences of cutting-edge innovation are often regressive when measured on a global scale. That is, the "haves" gain value and benefit from innovation as both the producers and consumers of such innovation while the "have-nots" are excluded. Understandably, then, the idea of "innovating for the Global South" is sometimes dismissed with great scepticism, if not outright derision.

In many respects, the contributors to this volume share this scepticism. By "innovating for the Global South" we do not mean introducing the most cutting-edge technologies or new, complex, and expensive interventions in health, employment, ecological sustainability, and economic productivity. In fact, many of the challenges faced by the poorest of the poor in the Global South, we contend, are simple challenges that can be mitigated with relatively simple fixes. We know, for example, that childhood anaemia can be reduced significantly if children receive an iron-fortified diet; that sanitation and access to clean water can be improved if fewer people practise defecation in the open; that seasonal or irregular wage earners are more likely to save money if they have access to simple savings mechanisms such as a bank account; that vaccination campaigns can be more effective if people have some form of identification; that the incidence of HIV/AIDS can be reduced if people are tested; that if given the option, parents would choose to have their children receive some schooling; and so on. However, *these simple problems can actually require very complex solutions*. Therefore, innovating for the Global South, as we see it in this volume, is fundamentally about innovating scalable solutions that mitigate the effects of poverty and underdevelopment in the Global South; it is not about inventing some new gizmo for some untapped market in the developing world.

Solutions to simple problems are complex because of the gap between the provision of an intervention (be it a technical aid, process fix, or organizational innovation), on the one hand, and the utilization of that intervention on the other. On the supply side, we need to ensure that technologies and processes intended to mitigate the effects of poverty in the Global South are appropriate to particular contexts. And yet, even the most well-thought-out fixes designed in the lab and tested in the field often yield very low utilization rates. Innovating for the Global South, therefore, is not limited to providing or supplying innovative fixes; it is not only a supply-side problem. On the demand side of the equation, consumers and end users, even when a practical solution is available, may choose, for a variety of reasons (discussed in this book), not to use or take up an otherwise well-designed product or intervention. Innovating for the Global South, therefore, requires finding ways to bridge the gap between supply and demand so that simple fixes to simple problems are in fact adopted, used, and sustained by those who would benefit from them. Innovations are the solutions. *Innovating*, however, is *the process* of discovery, trial, failure, adaptation, and, ultimately, implementation. This book is about the innovation process.

The Structure of This Book

The nine chapters in this book address the process of innovation from multiple vantage points. The authors of these chapters are scholars in the fields of medicine, economics, management, political science, engineering, and global health. They come to the same general question of innovating for the Global South with different methodological and intellectual lenses; yet they share common perspectives and collectively convey both innovation successes as well as the challenges that lie ahead.

The first two chapters establish the context in which the problem of innovating for the Global South needs to be evaluated. In chapter 1, Joseph Wong outlines the many background variables against which the innovation process needs to be understood. He makes a compelling point that in the Global South, the capitalist welfare state is increasingly unable to mitigate the effects of poverty and that innovating for the poor is not simply about reducing the cost of the product to the end user. This point is also underscored in chapter 2 by Dilip Soman, who paints a rich picture of the end user in the Global South using the lens of behavioural economics. He proposes that top-down innovation – when foisted upon an impoverished market – often fails because there is a fundamental disconnect between the innovator and the needs of the user. The chapter concludes with some specific prescriptions on how to make innovations behaviourally informed.

The next four chapters discuss various aspects of the "how to innovate" question. In chapter 3, Yu-Ling Cheng and Beverly Bradley introduce the notion of "appropriate technologies" – that is, technologies that are suited to the context in which they are expected to create value. Their chapter presents ways in which the appropriateness – and hence the value – of technology can be increased for those living in the Global South. In chapter 4, Rahim Rezaie makes the point that the traditional notion of innovation as a location-specific phenomenon is being replaced by the fragmentation and globalization of value chains. These disaggregated value chains create opportunities for countries and companies in the Global South to participate in the innovation process, allowing them not just to create value for the firms but to integrate the innovation process into the Global South.

In chapter 5, Anita McGahan, Rahim Rezaie, and Donald Cole propose a framework they call Embedded Innovations in Health, which puts the health and livelihood needs of the global poor at the centre of the innovations agenda and provides prescriptive recommendations on how to engage them actively in the innovation process. And in chapter 6, Ashley Aimone Phillips, Nandita Perumal, Carmen Ho, and Stanley Zlotkin use the domain of nutrition to develop a framework for scaling up innovations. They contend that while the need to scale up local innovations is shared among all stakeholders, knowledge translation and the sharing of scaling best practices among stakeholders remain constrained.

The last chapters discuss factors that facilitate the innovation process. In chapter 7, Murray Metcalfe provides a rich analytical overview of new financing models for the agenda of innovating for the global poor, and explores the implications of these cutting-edge financing models for the entire innovation system. In chapter 8, Janice Gross Stein argues that the established government policy practices and principles in foreign aid and development assistance will need to change going forward in order to integrate the innovation and redistribution agendas. She goes on to provide prescriptive advice for what governments can do to foster inclusive innovation. And finally, in chapter 9, Will Mitchell and Anita McGahan summarize the key themes in the book and present a research and policy agenda for the future.

The chapters in this book reflect the nature of the research being conducted by the Global Innovations Group at the University of Toronto. While this volume is written by academics and based on academic scholarship, it is aimed at a wider audience, from governments seeking to foster an innovative culture or to design suitable funding models to inventors and innovators trying to figure out how best to scale their innovation for social good, and from commentators to practitioners.

Many people have worked tirelessly behind the scenes to make this book project happen. Research assistants and support staff at the University of Toronto have helped us conduct the research reported on here and have provided editorial and other assistance. We would like to particularly thank Vandana Kumar at the India Innovation Institute for insightful comments, and Christine Heeah Lim and Katelyn Yoo at the

Rotman School of Management for editorial assistance and for managing the manuscript production process.

We would be remiss if we did not acknowledge the role that Lorna Jean Edmonds and Judith Wolfson played in encouraging the contributors of this book to collaborate with one another, and Cristina Amon, Roger Martin, Peter Paul, and Janice Stein in supporting the collaborations. Finaly, we thank Thulasidas Ravilla, Sankar and Divya Krishnan, Samuel Mathew, Nachiket Mor, the Canadian Trade Office in Taiwan, and Rajesh Chandy for facilitating and advising us on our field research.

We invite scholars, policy makers, and businesses – and, generally, anyone interested in encouraging innovations in the Global South – to engage with us in this important and exciting journey.

Joseph Wong and Dilip Soman, Toronto, May 2013

1

Poverty, Invisibility, and Innovation

JOSEPH WONG

Introduction

The global economy has grown by leaps and bounds over the past half-century. Driven by ever more open markets, increased international trade, and major technological advances, global productivity, and thus the accumulation of wealth, has benefited many. It is also the case, however, that many have not benefited from these global economic transformations. Inequality between countries continues to widen,[1] and contrary to the belief that aggregate growth leads to shared prosperity, inequality *within* countries has grown even more rapidly. With few exceptions, the Gini coefficient (the measure of inequality of income) has been on the rise around the world. If we consider, for instance, the distribution of individual (household) wealth globally, regardless of country, we can see that the share of wealth accounted for by the world's richest quintile grew from around 70 per cent in 1960 to 86 per cent by the end of the 1990s; meanwhile, the share of global wealth of the poorest 20 per cent decreased from an already paltry 2.3 per cent to just 1.1 per cent over the same period.[2]

The challenge of addressing socio-economic inequality is made even more difficult by the increasingly enduring nature of poverty. Wage disparities, particularly between workers employed in formal and secondary labour markets, as well as rising levels of unemployment globally, have contributed to increasingly chronic, if not permanent, poverty among the world's very poor; poverty is no longer a temporary or transitory phenomenon.[3] Under these circumstances, chances for social mobility are severely curtailed. The likelihood of finding regular work for those living in poverty is remote. Basic health, quality of life, productivity, access to education, and future life chances all suffer. The U.S. census refers to these conditions as "deep poverty." American sociologist William Julius Wilson views these realities as "extreme poverty." And Guy Standing characterizes this as the life of the "precariat," shorthand for the precarious proletariat.[4] Whatever labels one uses, the existential realities of chronic poverty – be it in the industrial North or the developing Global South – entail lived experiences and future prospects that are unimaginably bleak. The imperatives for social innovation – a new innovation agenda that improves the lives and life chances for the world's have-nots – could not be clearer.

Over the past few decades, the innovation agenda has taken centre stage nearly everywhere, in poor and rich countries alike. Governments are betting on the value-generating promise of cutting-edge technologies, industries, and services.[5] Firms and entrepreneurs are increasingly incentivized to get themselves into the innovation race, pitting their inventive knowledge against manufacturing brawn. And yet, until recently, the distributive consequences of innovation have been of secondary concern. As currently conceived, the goal of innovation is to be the first, the most novel, and the most cutting-edge in the field, with very little concern for who actually benefits from the innovation enterprise. It is to correct this omission that a *social innovation* agenda has emerged, focused specifically on innovating for poor people in order to increase their productivity, enhance their life chances, ensure their health, and, ultimately, provide them with opportunities to emerge from permanent poverty.

In very important ways, innovating for the poor is a supply-side problem. To enable poor people to benefit from innovative ideas and solutions, we need to be able to supply products, services, and interventions in affordable ways and forms. The idea of "frugal innovation," for instance, is typically understood as a supply-side challenge: that is, to supply accessible solutions to very poor people who would otherwise not be able to afford them. Several contributors to this volume address supply-side challenges in social innovation, and I join them in acknowledging the importance of innovating for the world's poor.

In this chapter, however, I argue that for a social innovation to be effective, the social innovation process and its outcomes need to be examined from the *perspective of the very poor*, or, to put it another way, through the lens of poverty. The key to social innovation is to understand the supply of social innovation as a source of value from the view of poor people, the end users. As Dean Karlan and Jacob Appel put it, "[i]f we want to solve poverty, we need to know what it is in real – not abstract – terms. We need to know how it smells, tastes and feels to the touch."[6] In this chapter, I begin by laying out a case for a new social innovation agenda, one that targets the poorest of the world's poor. I then outline a framework for examining the processes and impacts of potentially innovative solutions in order to provide a contextual background that sets the analytical stage for the other contributions in this volume.

Whither the World's Poor?

If we are concerned about the world's very poor, then it makes sense to ask who these people are and, further, where they live. Consider the proverbial "bottom billion," those who live on less than $1.25 (U.S.) per day. Though the absolute number of the world's bottom billion has decreased between 1988 and 2008, a more pronounced transformation has occurred with respect to the location of the world's poorest of the poor. In 1988, 93 per cent of all poor people (based on the $1.25 threshold) lived in low-income countries (LICs). By 2008, however, 72 per cent of the world's poor lived in middle-income countries (MICs). As Andy Sumner explains, since 2000, "over 700 million poor people have 'moved' into MICs by way of their countries' graduating from low income status." The most notable examples of this geographic shift are China and India, followed by Nigeria, Pakistan, and Indonesia. As Sumner reports, these five middle-income countries alone account for around two-thirds of the world's very poor.[7]

The implications of this geographic shift are twofold. First, while formerly poor countries have become much richer in the aggregate, people living within those countries have remained poor, in both an absolute and a relative sense. Second, and related to the first point, poverty and inequality are increasingly problems of *national redistribution rather than of facilitating aggregate economic growth*. While the conventional wisdom regarding development over the past few decades has held that making poor countries richer will ensure that poor people within those countries will in turn become less poor, the data, unfortunately, do not bear this out.

The challenge of redistribution is not new to us, however. We have become aware over the past century of both the normative and the instrumental importance of ensuring a relatively equitable distribution of wealth and economic opportunity within national societies. The invention of the capitalist welfare state, for example, is one of modern society's greatest innovations, legitimated further by the postwar pact of "embedded liberalism," a balanced mix of unfettered markets with Keynesian sensibilities. Notwithstanding typological differences among welfare regimes around the world (i.e., social democratic, social insurance, and liberal welfare states), the welfare state, in its most basic and crude formulation, entails public and private arrangements that protect workers employed in formal labour markets. The emergence of the welfare state reflected a certain kind of industrial capitalism at a certain moment in history, a particular era during which we saw the rise of the firm and the modern factory system and the development of labour unions representing the interests of wage-earning workers. The welfare state also enjoyed the fiscal and administrative capacity to extract surplus wealth from within society and to redistribute those resources, delivering social services, productivity-enhancing measures, and basic social protection for industrial workers. And as a political project, the welfare state idea proliferated because of the liberal democratic imperatives of moderating class interests among well-mobilized unions and social democratic parties, on the one hand, and the material interests of capital on the other. In short, the capitalist welfare state reflected a balance of political power resources among contending socio-economic interests.[8]

But while the challenges of redistribution are not new to us – and, indeed, the welfare state idea continues to appeal as a way of ensuring the delivery of both public and private interventions to mitigate the varied risks experienced by the poor – the reality is that the capitalist welfare state, a product of a certain political-economic phase of industrialization, has become an institutional anachronism. It is a model increasingly ill-suited to meet the challenges of inequality and poverty in the current age of global capitalism. Several reasons account for this.

First, we need to be reminded of the fact that the welfare state was intended to protect workers and not necessarily the poor. The various poor laws of the earlier industrial revolutions in Europe, and their lasting legacies today, reflect this institutional bias. Second, the capitalist welfare state, as an administrative apparatus, was not designed to protect all workers, but only those who were employed in formal labour markets. To deliver social welfare services and social protection required the state to have the administrative capacity to "see" – to borrow an idea from James Scott – its intended beneficiaries.[9] Employment in formal labour market jobs ensured this administrative visibility through workplace units and employers, the use of legal formal contracts, union rolls, and state-level fiscal mechanisms through which social services and other welfare interventions were administered. Currently, however, the majority of the world's workers are employed in informal sectors. In sub-Saharan Africa, approximately three-quarters of all workers (including those in the agricultural sector) are employed informally; the figure is about 70 per cent in South and Southeast Asia, and 50 per cent in Latin America. The informalization trend is not, I should add, unique to the agrarian developing world. For example, estimates reveal that since the 1990s over three-quarters of net job creation in the European Union has been in part-time employment and that employment in temporary (rather than full-time) work has grown ten times faster than overall employment.[10] The informalization of work – by which I mean precarious and flexible contracts, part-time work, self-employment, and seasonal wage earning – severely undermines the redistributive capacities of the welfare state.

Third, notwithstanding noble efforts by some to laud the autonomous spirit of informal work and declare marginality a myth, the reality is that informal workers are poor. The vast majority of workers in the Global South are employed in informal sectors, including those who are seasonal wage earners in the countryside and migrant workers, though they account for a relatively small share of national product. The disparity among the formal and informal is evident in rich countries as well. We know, for instance, that over a worker's lifetime in Japan, the non-standard worker typically earns just 22 per cent of the income of a standard, formal sector worker.[11] We also know that in South Korea, a rich country, self-employed workers, who make up nearly 40 per cent of the total workforce, earn on average 30 per cent less than their counterparts in the formal labour market.[12]

My point is simple: *poverty means invisibility*. The informalization of work has made those most in need of protection fiscally and administratively invisible to the welfare state. Poor people are politically marginalized, unable to mobilize resources to push for more social welfare measures, or even to have their voices heard. Critics of the welfare state note that the dualization of labour markets has contributed to the dualization of political activism among "insiders" (formally employed workers), who are represented by unions and their social democratic party allies, on the one hand, and "outsiders" (informally employed workers), who are more or less politically invisible, on the other.[13] Where the welfare state falls short with respect to mitigating the effects of inequality and poverty, the market has been slow to compensate. Endemic poverty and thus lower purchasing power among the very poor mean that the needs and demands of poor consumers have been by and large ignored by industry and the market.

Finally, the impoverished poor are physically invisible, unreachable by both the welfare state and the market. Consider what it means to live in a slum. Despite Millennium Development Goals initiatives to reduce the number of slum dwellers, several hundred million people continue to live in slums; these people are physically marginalized – spatially pushed out into the periphery and forgotten – sometimes by design.[14] Slum dwellers are, thus, invisible, often lacking any official identification; without regular work; considered illegal, "off the map," and without legal recourse. They live within a physical labyrinth of temporary and semi-permanent settlements without addresses, street names, or numbers; and they are continually on the move. As Arjun Appadurai observes, with reference to the slums of Mumbai, "a host of local, state-level and federal entities exist with a mandate to rehabilitate or ameliorate slum life. *But none of them knows exactly who the slum dwellers are, where they live or how they are to be identified.*"[15] Just imagine the practical obstacles of delivering social services to those most in need in these physical settings, to say nothing of the enormous stock of political will and entrepreneurial foresight required to reach them.

Poverty and Innovation

Social innovation, particularly innovating for the world's poor, is about making visible the otherwise invisible. Innovating for the poor is about the redistribution of resources, knowledge, and life-enhancing opportunities through governments and markets. A social innovation agenda must not, however, replicate the unsustainable and often precarious aims of philanthropy. The twentieth-century capitalist welfare state was an important and sustainable institutional innovation precisely because it was both equity enhancing and economically productive; an agenda to innovate for the poor must meet those same enduring objectives. Social innovations, if they are to be truly innovative, need to have an impact and be sustainable.

Drawing on the Schumpeterian notions of technological and social progress, we can describe innovation as the combination of invention and the generation of value. Leaving aside the specification of "value" for the moment, we see that the Schumpeterian understanding of innovation is important if we are to imagine social innovation as something more than philanthropic altruism. Innovation, if it is to have an impact and be sustainable, must *generate value.* An invention that produces no value is not innovative; it is merely a novelty, something new. Likewise, a product or service that generates value but does not involve anything new is also not an innovation. The keys to sustainable innovation are novelty *and* value.

Fortunately, as Wong and Soman note in the introductory chapter to this volume, the causes of many of the problems faced by the world's poorest of the poor today are not that complex. We know, for instance, that access to clean water and good nutrition drastically reduce infant mortality rates, just as maternal mortality can be curtailed if women have access to health facilities. We also know that if anti-malaria treated bed nets are used, then health outcomes, particularly among children, greatly improve. In other words, innovating for the poor is not about high-tech, cutting-edge invention. We already have, in many ways, the practical know-how. Where we need to be inventive and novel, however, is in how we produce, deliver, distribute, and encourage the utilization of potentially life-saving and life-enhancing interventions. Inventiveness in social innovation, in short, is about using existing knowledge to create new solutions.

We also have to be clear about what we mean by value. The materialist understanding of value is economic return on investment for the provider (i.e., revenues generated) and for the end user (i.e., economic productivity and wealth creation). The metric by which we measure such returns is quite simple. However, the value of social innovation, about which the primary concerns are the distributive consequences of novel invention, ought to be measured less by novelty and material value and more by social impact. Potentially socially innovative outputs need to be measured in terms of broader outcomes such as population health, economic opportunity, sustainability, and fairness and equity. Thus, from the perspective of the very poor, a socially innovative intervention creates value understood in terms of social impact.

The Aravind Eye Hospital

At the core of the social innovation agenda is the concept of a value proposition. Obviously from the point of view of the supplier (i.e., manufacturer, provider), the provision of a product or service must yield some measurable benefit, be it an economic return, a moral benefit, or both, as expressed by the idea of the "double bottom line" or taglines such as "profit for a purpose" or "doing well and doing good." As I stated previously, however, this chapter examines more specifically what makes a good value proposition, not exclusively from the perspective of the provider but also from the perspective of the end users, the very poor.

A good example of a socially innovative organization is the Aravind Eye Hospital (AEH), a non-profit eye-care hospital in the southern Indian state of Tamil Nadu. It is well known that of the 45 million blind people in the world, a significant number of them (about 20 per cent) live in India. Many, if not most, of these incidences of blindness can be cured with early diagnosis, regular check-ups, and, if needed, cataract surgery. In fact, much of the world's blindness is "needless blindness." The AEH has played a critical role in eradicating blindness in India, and its model of eye care delivery has also been instrumental in eliminating needless blindness in other parts of the developing world, as hospitals elsewhere emulate the AEH system. Between 1976, when the AEH was founded, to 2005, the hospital and the screening camps it organizes have processed more than 20 million outpatient cases and performed 2.5 million cataract surgeries. The key to the AEH's success is its ability to reduce the cost per surgery. Whereas in most Western health-care systems a cataract surgery is typically reimbursed at around $3,000, the AEH is able to perform the surgery at one-hundredth of the cost, for just $30 per surgery.

As with all innovative solutions, the AEH is an integration of multiple innovations, some technological and some organizational. Organizationally, the AEH works on a high patient throughput model of care. The surgical theatre is equipped with two operating stations. As one patient is being operated on, the other bed is being prepped for the next patient. When the first patient's cataract operation is completed, the surgeon immediately begins to operate on the next. Each cataract surgery takes, on average, ten minutes. High patient throughput means high volume, reducing the cost per surgery. To ensure such a high patient throughput, however, the Aravind hospital must generate demand for eye screens and, if needed, cataract surgery. To that end, the AEH organizes eye screening camps in surrounding villages. The AEH pre-announces the screening camp, brings buses to the village, conducts eye examinations for free, and then brings those villagers who require surgery back to the hospital. The AEH organizes approximately 1,300 eye camps each year, and has conducted more than 100 million eye exams since 1976. Aravind eye camps account for nearly half of all cataract surgeries performed by the AEH.

The AEH has also innovated on the technological front. In 1992, the AEH established Aurolab, its medical equipment manufacturing arm. Located near the main hospital in Madurai, Aurolab makes, at a very low cost, tools, sutures, and intraocular lenses for cataract surgery. When Aurolab was founded during the early 1990s, the cost for intraocular lenses manufactured by foreign firms was about $120 U.S. per pair; the Aurolab is able to manufacture its own lenses for just $6. The fact that Aurolab lenses have been approved by international regulatory bodies for sale and distribution in foreign markets is evidence that the AEH's efforts at cost reduction have not compromised quality. More generally, outcomes data comparing the AEH's record against that of the British Ophthalmological Society show that the AEH's performance is as effective as that of its British counterparts, if not more so.[16]

That the AEH is able to reduce the cost per surgery through scale efficiencies from high patient volumes, continual demand generation, and the lower costs of labour and surgical materials has meant that nearly two-thirds of all surgeries are performed at no cost to the patient (either free of charge or subsidized by government insurers). In terms of financing innovation, the AEH makes little distinction between fee-paying and non-fee-paying patients in order to mitigate any social stigma among those who can or cannot afford to pay. All patients, regardless of whether they are fee-paying or non-fee-paying, have the same surgery, performed by the same surgeon, and, unless otherwise specified, receive the same intraocular lens. The only difference is in the level of personal comfort during pre-operative and post-operative care: fee-paying patients recover in an air-conditioned private room, while those who are non-fee-paying recover in a multi-patient, non-air-conditioned ward.[17] Either way, the poor patient and the patient who is able to pay both regain their sight at the AEH.

This simple objective – regaining one's sight – is the AEH's core value proposition to the prospective patient. From the perspective of a blind person, the prospect of being able to see brings tremendous benefit and, broadly speaking, tremendously good value. In this respect, though the AEH is an inspiring model of sustainable and high-impact social innovation, it is also, in many ways, the proverbial "easy case." That being said, the example of the AEH nonetheless highlights important insights and lessons about how effective social innovations are when viewed as net-beneficial value propositions from the perspective of the very poor. Three points stand out. First, the AEH demonstrates the importance of *cost-reduction*, significantly reducing the cost burden to the very poor end user. Second, the fact that the AEH minimizes distinctions between fee-paying and non-fee-paying patients reveals how the AEH reduces other *transaction costs of utilization*, such as social stigmatization, that might otherwise discourage a patient from seeking care. Third, efforts by the AEH to educate, screen, transport, and treat patients show how the organization *actively generates demand* for its services. The eye screening camps, for example, are intended to stimulate demand among patients who would otherwise likely choose not to seek care or not have the opportunity to do so. These three points – reduced cost, reduced transaction costs, and demand generation – are discussed in further detail below.

Cost

We know that most consumers are price sensitive; very poor consumers, however, are *very price sensitive*. Our end user probably lives on less than $2 per day. If he lives in the countryside, he is likely a seasonal and irregular wage earner, meaning there are weeks, sometimes months, when there is no income. If she is from the city, there is a very strong likelihood that she lives illegally in a slum dwelling. For someone who lives incredibly close to the proverbial "margin," the perception of risk is near-term; immediate benefits are far more important than long-term ones. Our end user also likely lives far from any proper health facility. Nutritional intake is probably very poor. And it is likely that our end user is without any official identification and thus without access to government support. Under these conditions, socially innovative solutions must reduce the cost of utilization and adoption to the end user; otherwise he or she will likely choose not to utilize the product or service, no matter how beneficial it is purported to be.

Cost reduction is a key determinant of whether a particular intervention, product, or service is seen to be a source of value from the perspective of the very poor. Field studies show, for example, that when it comes to the adoption of new health products, such as anti-malaria treated bed nets, price is the single most important variable. Because poor people have so few surplus resources, they experience what Pascaline Dupas calls "liquidity constraints." Not surprisingly, then, take-up rates correlate strongly with household income.[18] In a related study, Dupas finds that the provision of short-run subsidies for the purchase of treated bed nets increases a household's long-run adoption of the product. The inference here is that when the initial cost of utilization is offset, over the longer term the realized benefits (i.e., better health, more productivity, and so on) come to outweigh the material costs of continuing to use the bed nets. Learning is important, Dupas concludes, but cost reduction to the end user, at least initially, is critical for utilization.[19]

Subsidies are one way to reduce the cost of utilization for the end user; another is simply to reduce the price to the consumer. For instance, the One Laptop Per Child (OLPC) initiative, and more recently the Aakash computing tablet, are high-profile examples of how existing technological platforms can be stripped down functionally to reduce the cost of production, from which the savings are passed on to the consumer or adopter. General Electric, in its efforts to tap into new markets in the developing world, has engineered and produced a portable, handheld, ultrasound machine that is capable of performing most simple applications. That it costs less than 15 per cent of GE's high-end machines means that it has been adopted and used by health-care providers in rural parts of the Global South.[20] Abdallah Daar and Peter Singer showcase several examples of innovative firms and organizations in the Global South that have, through the inventive talents of local entrepreneurs, health-care providers, and engineers, been able to drastically reduce the costs to a fraction of the First World prices for specific medical treatments, prosthetics, surgeries, information technologies hardware, and essential medicines and vaccines.[21]

Cost is obviously a critical factor with respect to whether a poor person perceives a proposition to be good value or to provide a net benefit when utilized. Clearly, if the cost to the end user is too high, then the probability of take-up or adoption is low. That being said, cost reduction alone is not enough to ensure utilization. We know, for instance, that even when HIV tests are free, take-up rates, especially among men, remain low for fear of social ostracism. Pre-measured micro-nutrient powders, even when free or heavily subsidized for the end user, are unevenly distributed among countries, with acceptance being far from universal. The Tata Nano, an automotive frugal-engineering feat that promises to bring the mobility of automobile travel to even the poorest of the poor, has not sold well even though it is priced very affordably. There are clearly other variables at work here, other "transaction costs" that need to be accounted for in determining good value propositions for the very poor.

Other Transaction Costs

During a research trip to India, I visited a rural health-care facility that provided diagnostic screens at minimal cost to rural Indian villagers. Though great care was taken in predetermining what type of screening would be most effective for that particular village (following an initial epidemiological survey of the area population), the take-up rate for the diagnostic screens was unexpectedly low. It was unexpected because conventional wisdom tells us that diagnostic screens are an economical, cost-effective way to treat potentially catastrophic conditions at an early stage, with significant benefits to patients' long-term health. And yet, even though villagers were educated about these benefits, utilization rates continued to be low and decreased quite rapidly after the initial period of subsidized tests had ended.

How do we explain the villagers' counter-intuitive behaviour? First, not surprisingly, the cost to the patient of the screen is a critical determinant of utilization. Even relatively inexpensive tests are too costly for many of the very poor. Second, the time taken off work in order to travel to the clinic created a significant opportunity cost for villagers who rely on seasonal wages; the need to make repeated visits to the clinic compounded this additional cost. And third, the idea that one needed to be screened for something for which the best-case scenario is that nothing is wrong made little sense to the villager, while the fact that, if something was discovered to be wrong, unaffordable follow-up treatment would be needed was an additional deterrent. The notion of early detection to mitigate long-term health and economic risks is thus not viewed as a particularly good value proposition by the villager, whose primary concerns are considerably more near-term and immediate. The point is that the costs of utilization, broadly defined, are not limited to the price to the end user of the intervention itself – in this case a relatively cheap diagnostic screening test – but include additional transaction costs such as the opportunity costs of lost time from work and the medical care costs of long-term treatment. When these additional costs to the end user are factored in, an intervention such as a diagnostic screen is not considered a particularly good value proposition.

If we evaluate the effectiveness of social innovation as a value proposition to the prospective end user, then additional transaction costs, as I describe them here, are costs that exceed (or add onto) the consumer price of a specific product or service. The greater the additional transaction costs, the less likely that a potential solution will be used. Some of these transaction costs are material. We know, as the example of rural health care in India demonstrates, that travel costs are often prohibitive for very poor people. In addition, the opportunity costs of time lost from work and wages, whether for a day or even only a few hours, can be significant. This means that even if the price of an otherwise effective health-care intervention, public health campaign, educational tool, or agricultural innovation can be zeroed out – that is, provided free – additional *material* transaction costs will deter poor people from accessing or using them.

Other transaction costs to the end user are less material (or economic) but more social and cultural in nature (see Yu-Ling Cheng and Beverley Bradley's chapter on appropriate technologies, as well as the chapter by McGahan, Rezaie, and Cole on embedded innovation). We know, for instance, that because of gender dynamics within the patriarchal household, utilization rates are lower for micro-credit schemes that require wives and mothers to leave the home. Free condom distribution campaigns to stem the spread of HIV/AIDS, we have learned, are often underused because of cultural norms of masculinity in sexual relationships. We also know that potentially beneficial interventions that disrupt socially ingrained behaviours – such as nutrition fortification in daily diets, the collection of water, or even the use of a sit-down toilet – tend not to be adopted or are resisted.

We also know that trust and credibility are critical for the adoption and utilization of socially innovative solutions and that the absence of such social norms deters adoption. Studies on HIV counselling and testing in the developing world show that cost reduction in the testing procedure actually has little effect on uptake; rather, confidentiality, convenience (door-to-door testing), and the credibility (and accuracy) of the blood test – all indicators related to trust – are far better predictors of utilization.[22] Jishnu Das and Saumya Das similarly show that villagers are far more likely to participate in vaccination campaigns when the observable benefits are quick and when the individual patient has had previous positive interactions with the health-care provider, even if for an unrelated matter.[23] Just as trust enhances a value proposition from the perspective of the end user, the absence of trust makes such a value proposition much less attractive. For example, field reports from India tell us that one cause of the uneven utilization rates for the rural employment guarantee scheme, an otherwise generous program intended to provide work for those without it, is localized corruption surrounding work projects and compensation that even includes tampering with the muster rolls.[24] Corruption – or the absence of trust – creates an additional transaction cost for an otherwise highly beneficial employment guarantee program.

My point is that reducing the material cost – the consumer price – of any potentially innovative solution for a pressing social problem is not enough to ensure widespread adoption and utilization. Price is, of course, a critical dimension to providing good value to the end user. But there are many other transaction costs that need to be addressed if we are to "sell" an idea, product, or service as a good value proposition to the very poor.

Generating Demand

An important challenge for realizing the full impact of potentially so-cially innovative solutions is generating demand for such solutions. A good value proposition should generate demand. However, we too of-ten presume that latent demand for something that should benefit poor people will automatically be taken up. After all, one might ask, who does not want access to clean water or a sanitary toilet that in turn pro-vides a new source of usable energy? Who would choose to stay blind if they could see? Who does not want to see their children healthy, hap-py, and learning? And yet, *the presumption of latent demand necessarily resulting in active demand is a false premise.*

In our visit to the Aravind Eye Hospital (AEH), for example, we learned that when a patient is diagnosed with cataracts at an AEH eye screening camp, the hospital provides that patient with lunch and im-mediately loads the patient onto the bus to be taken back to the surgical hospital in Madurai. Why such measures? It was explained that though patients are assured that they will regain their sight (often free of charge), if they are left to go home, even just to have a meal or to pack for an overnight stay at the hospital, many will not return to the bus to be taken to the hospital for surgery. The presumption of latent demand for what is obviously a great value proposition – the ability to see – does not guar-antee an active demand for cataract surgery. In the case of the AEH and its patient recruitment strategy, the generation of active demand is in fact somewhat coerced. Consider also the Tata Nano, another example that illustrates the gap between the presumption of latent demand, on the one hand, and active demand, on the other. Tata designed its ultra-affordable car precisely with the low-income market in mind. In fact, Tata marketed the Nano as the automotive solution for poor people. The initial sales campaign for the car, however, was a disaster. Poor people shunned the Nano precisely because of the social stigma attached to the notion that it was the car *for* the very poor. The example of the Tata Nano demonstrates how latent demand for affordable transport does not necessarily translate into active demand for an inexpensive car.

Active demand, therefore, needs to be generated. To put it another way, from the perspective of the end user, the perception that a particular product, service, or intervention is a good value proposition needs to be created, even manipulated. M-Pesa, a mobile banking system introduced in Kenya, is an excellent example of generating active demand for a socially innovative service. The M-Pesa system, introduced by Vodacom's local subsidiary, Safaricom, works with local banks to provide a mobile banking system. M-Pesa provides an "e-float," a virtual account balance tied to a real bank that can be used to save money and to conduct financial transactions in real time. Introduced in 2007, the M-Pesa system has already enrolled 14 million users (out of a population of about 40 million) and accounts for transaction volumes equal to one-third of Kenya's GDP. Over 75 per cent of survey respondents report that they are "extremely happy" with the M-Pesa service (rating it at 9 or 10 on a 10-point scale), and 96 per cent of respondents indicate that they would experience a negative impact if M-Pesa were to shut down. Clearly M-Pesa has deeply penetrated the personal banking market and has positioned its service as virtually indispensable. In short, M-Pesa has generated and sustained enormous demand for its mobile banking service.[25] How did it do this, and what lessons can be distilled from the M-Pesa case?

Above all else, the M-Pesa service addresses an important need. Prior to its introduction, the vast majority of Kenyans were "unbanked." This was highly problematic for many. Kenya is a poor country rife with poverty, where incomes are precarious and household savings are low. For many, carrying cash is extremely dangerous, yet few Kenyans had access to banks, in part because the banking infrastructure was terribly underdeveloped, in part because most did not trust the banks. The M-Pesa system thus met this latent demand for a more secure means of saving money and conducting financial transactions. To reduce cost to the end user, the M-Pesa banking system leveraged existing technologies. Mobile phone technology had already penetrated the Kenyan market. Moreover, M-Pesa is built upon an old SMS technology, meaning virtually any mobile handset is compatible with the e-banking system.

In many ways, the M-Pesa model was an innovative idea. It was efficient and useful. It leveraged existing technologies and repurposed old technologies, thus lowering the cost of adoption. But M-Pesa also actively generated demand for its services. Before it became the multi-functional, multi-service banking system that it now is, M-Pesa was initially rolled out as a simple solution for urban workers to send remittances back home to their families in the countryside. By initially focusing only on the remittances business, M-Pesa was able to generate market demand among relatively well-to-do urban workers, providing them with a safe and reliable way to send money home. In so doing, the remittances business model also ensured that poorer market segments – specifically, people living in the countryside and receiving remittances – were required to enrol in the M-Pesa mobile banking system. By generating demand in one market, M-Pesa actively generated demand in another, selling the service as a good value proposition for diverse market segments. Furthermore, M-Pesa purposely marketed the mobile banking system to middle-class wage earners living and working in the cities, deliberately eschewing the perception that its affordable services were intended for low-tech, low-income users in the countryside. M-Pesa thus strategically marketed its banking system as an aspirational – yet attainable – service, thereby avoiding the social stigma associated with other products and services, such as the Tata Nano, that explicitly target the very poor. Consequently, M-Pesa was able to generate quick, widespread, and sustained demand among otherwise diverse markets.

Conclusion

Andy Sumner writes that we need to rethink our development strategies, to move our focus from "poor countries to poor people."[26] Though he is writing with specific reference to foreign development aid and assistance, Sumner nonetheless points to the key challenge in mitigating the effects of poverty around the world: it is no longer solely a problem of generating aggregate growth among poor countries but instead a complex problem of redistribution for poor people in all countries, rich or poor. But how do we do this? This chapter, by viewing the problem of redistribution and innovation from the perspective of the poor, highlights key factors that need to be considered. The unique existential realities of poverty shape how very poor people make welfare decisions. Cost to the end user is clearly a key deciding factor. But lowering cost is not the only imperative, as empirical studies have shown. Other "transaction costs," both material (opportunity costs) and non-material (social-cultural), imposed upon the poor end user matter as well. And finally, active demand for potentially innovative solutions needs to be generated; the presumption of latent demand is a false premise. In sum, this chapter has focused on the demand side of the social innovation equation, an important though under-studied dimension of the distributive implications of innovation. The contributions that follow in this volume build upon the insights introduced in this chapter.

THE IDEA IN BRIEF

The capitalist welfare state is increasingly unable to mitigate the effects of poverty, especially in the developing world. Innovating for the poor, to be successful, requires not only attention to ways of reducing cost to the end user but also novel efforts to reduce other transaction costs of utilization and to generate demand for potentially beneficial solutions.

IMPLICATIONS

1 Creating solutions to mitigate poverty requires that providers (including policy makers, firms, and civil society organizations) understand the conditions of extreme poverty.
2 Innovative solutions for poverty must be viewed as a good value proposition – a source of net benefit – from the perspective of the end user.
3 Providers must give equal consideration to (i) consumer price, (ii) other transaction costs incurred by utilization, and (iii) the generation of demand for potentially innovative solutions.

FOOD FOR THOUGHT

Are there general, law-like observations that we can make about how poor people everywhere – Global South and North, urban and rural – make decisions about their individual welfare?

REFERENCES

1 Birdsall, Nancy. (1998). "Life is unfair: Inequality in the world." *Foreign Policy* 111 (Summer).

2 United Nations Development Programme. (1999). *Human development report*. New York and Oxford: Oxford University Press.
3 Emmenegger, P., Hausermann, S., Palier, B., & Seeleib-Kaiser, M. (2012). "How we grow unequal." In Emmenegger, Hausermann, Palier, & Seeleib-Kaiser (Eds), *The age of dualization: The changing face of inequality in deindustrializing societies.* Oxford: Oxford University Press; and Rueda, D. (2007). *Social democracy inside out: Government partisanship, insiders, and outsiders in industrialized democracies.* Oxford: Oxford University Press.
4 Standing, Guy. (2011). *The precariat: The new dangerous class.* London: Bloomsbury Academic.
5 Wong, Joseph. (2011). *Betting on biotech: Innovation and the limits of Asia's developmental state.* Ithaca, NY: Cornell University Press.
6 Karlan, D., & Appel, J. (2011). *More than good intentions: Improving the way the world's poor borrow, save, farm, learn, and stay healthy.* New York: Penguin Group, 37.
7 Sumner, Andy. (2011). "The new bottom billion: What if most of the world's poor live in middle-income countries?" *CGD Brief.* Center for Global Development (March): 1.
8 Esping-Andersen, Gosta. (1992). *Three worlds of welfare capitalism.* Princeton, NJ: Princeton University Press; and Korpi, Walter. (1983). *The democratic class struggle.* Boston: Routledge.
9 Scott, James. (1998). *Seeing like a state: How certain schemes to improve the human condition have failed.* New Haven, CT: Yale University Press.
10 Hausermann, S., & Schwande, H. (2011). "Varieties of dualization? Labor market segmentation and insider-outsider divides across regimes." In Emmenegger et al. (Eds), *The age of dualization*, 29.
11 Cited in Lee, Seung-Yoon. (2011). "Re-defining work in post-industrial East Asia: A literature review and research outline." Unpublished paper.
12 Jones, Randall S. (2009). *Reforming the tax system in Korea to promote economic growth and cope with rapid population aging.* OECD Economics Department Working Paper, No. 671: 7.
13 See Emmenegger et al. (Eds) (2011), *The age of dualization;* see also Rueda, David. (2005). "Insider-outsider politics in industrialized democracies: The challenge to social democratic parties." *American Political Science Review* 99 (February).
14 David, Mike. (2007). *Planet of slums.* Brooklyn & London: Verso.
15 Appadurai, Arjun. (2002). "Deep democracy: Urban governmentality and the horizon of politics." *Public Culture* 14 (1).
16 Singer, Peter. (2010). *The end of the accord: What can Canada learn from the developing world about the affordability of healthcare?* Medical Research Council for Global Health, University of Toronto (July).

17 The Aravind Eye Hospital, facing increasing competition from similar hospitals in the eye-care sector, has begun to differentiate its services more in order to capture higher-fee-paying customers.

18 Dupas, Pascaline. (2009). "What matters (and what does not) in households' decision to invest in malaria prevention?" *American Economic Review: Papers and Proceedings* 99 (2): 228.

19 Dupas, Pascaline. (2010). "Short-run subsidies and long-run adoption of new health products: Evidence from a field experiment." *BREAD* (Bureau of Research and Economic Analysis of Development) *Working Paper No. 258* (May).

20 Immelt, J., Govindarajan, V., & Trimble, C. (2009). "How GE is disrupting itself." *Harvard Business Review* (October).

21 Daar, A., & Singer, P. (2011). *The grandest challenge: Taking life-saving science from lab to village*. Toronto: Random House.

22 Angotti, N., Bula, A., Gaydosh, L., Kimchi, E.Z., Thornton, R.L., & Yeatman, S.E. (2009). "Increasing the acceptability of HIV counseling and testing with three C's: Convenience, confidentiality and credibility." *Social Science & Medicine* 68 (12) (June).

23 Das, J., & Das, S. (2003). "Trust, learning and vaccination: A case study of a north Indian village." *Social Science & Medicine* 57 (1) (July).

24 See Jha, R., Gaiha, R., & Shankar, S. (2010). "National rural employment guarantee programme in Andhra Pradesh and Rajasthan: Some recent evidence." *Contemporary South Asia* 18 (2); Dreze, J., & Khera, R. (2009). "The battle for employment guarantee." *Frontline* 26 (1); and Chakraborty, Pinaki. (2007). "Implementation of employment guarantee: A preliminary appraisal." *Economic & Political Weekly* (17 February).

25 See, for instance, Jack, W., & Suri, T. (2010). "The economics of M-PESA." Unpublished paper.

26 Sumner (2011), "The new bottom billion," 2.

2

Behaviourally Informed Innovation

DILIP SOMAN

> If a man write a better book, preach a better sermon, or make a better mouse-trap than his neighbor, though he build his house in the woods, the world will make a beaten path to his door.
>
> – Ralph Waldo Emerson[1]

Despite the quoted assertion of Ralph Waldo Emerson (which has often been simplified to "Build a better mousetrap and the world will beat a path to your door"), it is well established that the success rates for innovations and new products are low irrespective of whether the innovations are indeed better than what the marketplace has to offer. In the United States, recent estimates suggest that as many as 75 per cent of all new product launches could be considered as relative failures.[2] Failure rates range between 40 and 90 per cent as a function of product category, and these failure rates have not changed with time. Examples of innovative products and services that promised a revolution in the way consumers in the Global North would lead their lives but that failed to deliver on their promise include online grocery shopping services like Webvan, TiVo, the electric car, and the Sacagawea gold coin. In the Global South, one of the key challenges to innovations is the lack of scale; innovations that work well in a narrow, focused context fail to scale both horizontally in the Global South as well as vertically in other parts of the developed world.[3] Why have we not seen successful innovative products and processes like M-Pesa in Kenya and Tanzania or the Aravind Eye Hospital in India spreading widely around the globe?

Why do innovations not succeed as much as we would like them to? A number of reasons have been offered for this lack of success. These typically include supply-side factors such as a shortfall of investments, a desire to launch the product too soon, improper competitive analysis, and insufficient market research. In much of this rationalization, the "better mousetrap" argument is still the prevailing underlying theme, and it can be loosely paraphrased as follows: "We know we have a better product and consumers should indeed see the value in it; we just need to work harder to communicate and demonstrate the value." This chapter argues that this line of thinking is fundamentally flawed. In particular, I contend that top-down innovation – say, a new product that is invented in a laboratory detached from the context and conditions in which a consumer is actually going to use it – results in a disconnect between the views of the innovator and the response of the user. The disconnect stems from the fact that innovators have a poor understanding of the psychology of the adoption and usage decisions made by the consumer. Innovators, policy makers, and businesses have long viewed the consumer as an entity that maximizes self-interest, that recognizes value (utility), that is forward looking and unemotional, and that has the ability to make the necessary computations in arriving at a utility-maximizing choice. Research in the field of behavioural economics suggests that this view might be flawed.

Indeed, recent research has implicitly argued that efforts at solving social problems related to poverty, education, hunger, and public health – or at solving personal and household problems related to savings rates, eating disorders, and healthy lifestyles – have focused too narrowly on developing solutions and not sufficiently on developing a rich understanding of the process that individuals use to adopt those solutions.[4] Mullainathan refers to this imbalance between the work done on innovation creation and the work done on innovation adoption as the "last mile problem," a term borrowed from the field of telecommunications. The "last mile" refers to the final leg of delivering connectivity from a communications provider to a customer, and it is often considered to be the weakest link because of the complexities involved in physically reaching a vast and widely dispersed body of end users.

Implementing socially innovative programs and products also presents an interesting "last mile" challenge. Typically, this challenge is a problem of psychology – people are reluctant to adopt positive behaviours and useful products because of biased beliefs, the complexities of choice, self-control problems, and perceptual errors.[5] Psychological factors sometimes drive decision making to a greater extent than economic factors. In a recent demonstration in the consumer credit market, Bertrand and colleagues showed that psychological variables (like the presence of a photograph on a loan offer letter) played a significant role in decisions to take up loan offers relative to more functional variables.[6]

The First Mile and the Last: Two Examples

Consider two examples that illustrate the idea of the last mile problem more concretely. The Canada Learning Bond (CLB) is a grant offered by the Government of Canada to enable parents, friends, and family members in families with modest incomes to start saving early for the postsecondary education of their children.[7] Viewed from a purely economic perspective, the CLB represents $500 of free money for eligible families to be applied towards education expenses. As such, the take-up rate for the CLB should be close to 100 per cent. Unfortunately, at the end of 2011, the number was only in the 16 to 19 per cent range. The standard "better mousetrap" proponents would suggest that the low adoption rates could be explained by a lack of awareness of the program; however, our interviews suggest that there are many other reasons. Some eligible families did not have a bank account (as was required to enrol in the program); or they found the application forms too complex; or they felt out of place in a formal banking environment; or they had language issues that made them feel uncomfortable talking with the appropriate personnel. Work done by community agencies to address these "last mile" challenges has gone a long way towards improving the adoption rate of the CLB.

A second example is based on the research of Eric Johnson and Dan Goldstein[8] into organ donation programs. They documented the effective consent rates (i.e., the percentage of eligible citizens who had indicated their intention to donate organs and/or tissue after their death) across a number of European countries and reported a fairly interesting pattern of data: consent rates were either fairly low (in the 4 to 27 per cent range) for some countries or extremely high (in the 85 to 99.98 per cent range) for others, with virtually no European country reporting a consent rate in the middle of the range. Even when controlling for several "first mile" variables such as transplant infrastructure, expenditures on programs, economic and educational status, and religion, the differences among the consent rates were large and seemingly puzzling. The differences were due to the default assumptions. For example, the default assumption in the United Kingdom (17 per cent consent rate) is that individuals must opt in to the program (typically by filling in the forms to register themselves). In contrast, the default assumption in Austria (99.98 per cent consent rate) is that all individuals will donate organs unless they opt out by filling in the requisite forms and petitioning to get their names taken off the registry. Defaults have been shown to have large effects in a number of different domains and to be effective for two reasons. First, defaults suggest a social norm – so a default assumption of "everyone donates organs" signals that it is the appropriate thing to do and might increase the perceived value of that option. Second, humans are inherently lazy, and the perceived cost of the effort required to move away from the default might not seem worth it.

The Psychology of the Last Mile: Insights from Behavioural Psychology and Economics

The field of behavioural economics paints a picture of a consumer that is dramatically different from the one painted by the field of economics. A consumer who follows the assumptions of economics has the ability to recognize a better mousetrap when she sees one, has the motivation to adopt it and try it, has the sophistication to compute her willingness to pay for it, and has the foresight to adopt the mousetrap today even in situations where the benefits will only be seen at a later point in time. As the examples of the Canada Learning Bond and organ donations suggest, real consumers are different. Real consumers are emotional, use intuition to make decisions, are lazy (both physically and cognitively), and are systematically influenced by the context in making decisions. A number of findings from behavioural economics shed light on the manner in which decisions are made in real life.

1 *The Construction of Value*: The first challenge to the belief that consumers can assess and quantify value comes from Mark Twain's *The Adventures of Tom Sawyer*. In the narrative, Tom has played hookey from school and as punishment is given the laborious task of painting

a fence on a hot day while his friends are walking by to play. In a fit of inspiration, Tom starts painting the fence with a great gusto and energy, compelling his friends to ask why he is so upbeat. The rest of the narrative is simple yet thought-provoking – Tom claimed he was having a lot of fun painting, allowed his disbelieving friends who wanted a try to do so if they paid him, and pretty soon Tom's friends were painting for him and paying him for the privilege. Tom Sawyer, with some simple reframing, had converted something that had a negative utility to something that people were willing to pay money for. Most modern-day consumers are a lot like Tom's friends and are unable to place dollar tags on consumption opportunities unless there is a well-established market norm.[9]

2 *Losses and Gains*: Much of the early research in behavioural economics by Daniel Kahneman and Amos Tversky centred on the psychology of losses and gains. These researchers proposed prospect theory as the model that explained the manner in which consumers perceive monetary (and, indeed, more generally, all numerical) outcomes.[10] The theory contends that people value outcomes with reference to some neutral reference point, with the result that outcomes are coded as gains or losses. For example, a consumer looking to adopt a new innovation might look at the price of the closest substitute as a reference point. If the reference point was $100 and the price of the new innovation is $120, a loss of $20 would be coded. On the other hand, if the price is $80, it would be a gain of $20. However, the behaviourally insightful feature of the prospect theory is the claim that people overweigh losses by a factor of 2.25 relative to gains. For instance, the pain associated with a loss of $20 is 2.25 times the happiness associated with the gain of $20. In other words, in any transaction, gains need to be significantly greater than losses for that transaction to be seen as worthwhile. This behavioural property – loss aversion – leads to another robust phenomenon called the endowment effect. The endowment effect simply states that the value people assign to objects and products they possess is greater than the value they assign to identical objects and products that they do not possess.

3 *The Status Quo Bias*: The status quo bias (also referred to as inertia or laziness) refers to the fact that people tend to stick with the current product, course of action, or outcome even when a better alternative exists. One explanation of the status quo bias is the finding from the prospect theory about the psychological value of losses relative to gains. Interestingly, recent evidence suggests that the status quo bias

intensifies with time – the longer that people stay with the default option, the greater the likelihood that they will continue to do so. The status quo bias explains why investors tend to hold on to financial assets when it is clearly sub-optimal to do so.

4 *The Role of Context*: A traditional approach to innovations would suggest that a better mousetrap is better under all conditions. A behavioural approach would suggest that the value of the mousetrap depends on the context of the decision. Consider the research on the compromise effect, which suggests that when consumers are unsure of preferences and are offered an assortment of three options that vary in price and quality, they tend to choose the option in the middle.[11] For example, a car shopper who is given three options – the low-priced basic model with no extras, a high-priced fully loaded model with all the extras, and a mid-priced model with some extras – will most likely choose the middle option. Likewise, coffee shops selling coffee in three sizes (small, medium, and large) report that the most popular size of coffee is the medium size. Interestingly, it does not matter how much coffee is in the medium cup – what matters is the fact that it is in the middle. Further, consumers do not have a very clear intuition that the context is affecting their choices.

Taken together with the earlier example of defaults and the claim that consumers might not have the cognitive sophistication to evaluate the utility of innovations, it is apparent that the consumers' preferences may be shaped by what the context signals to them. In the case of the compromise effect, the context might push the average consumer into a mindset of "I want to avoid the extremes so I will stick to what is in the middle." In the case of defaults, the context signals what a socially acceptable norm might be, and in other situations the availability or popularity of certain products could serve as a signal of their quality. More generally, it would be fair to conclude that consumers might infer what they want as a function of what is available and how it is presented to them.

5 *Information and Disclosure*: The tenets of economics assume that the more information consumers are given, the more well-informed and hence optimal their choices will be. Likewise, it is assumed that the more options consumers are given, the more likely they are to find an option that meets their needs. However, recent research shows that both of these assumptions might be flawed.[12] In domains ranging from standard packaged goods (jams, analgesics) to retirement savings plans, researchers have found that adding more alternatives

increases the cognitive complexity of the choice task. As a result, consumers may (a) choose using simplified heuristics (e.g., "I'll buy whatever I bought last time"), (b) keep changing choices over time as they are unsure of which option is the best, or (c) choose not to choose. The last outcome can be particularly undesirable in domains where the product or project goal is to get people to engage in socially or individually desirable behaviours. For example, studies have shown that people do not join retirement savings plans because there are too many options.[13] Providing excessive information can also have deleterious effects on the quality of choices made by making the choice process cognitively complex.

6 *Mental Accounting*:[14] The basic premise of mental accounting is the idea that people do not treat money as fungible but rather tend to label it, and that the labelling of money influences the manner in which the money is spent.[15] The fact that people tend to label money has been extensively documented in the literature. In particular, Zelizer[16] has shown that people partition their money into groups as a function of what they plan to do with it – for instance, "money for paying bills" is different from "fun money" or "pin money." Another way consumers track their financial activities is to label their money based on the context in which it was obtained. In a variant of mental accounting called "income accounting," labels are determined by the money's source. Research also suggests that there may be a match between the source of the funds and how they are used. For instance, money won in a football betting pool is used for dining at a restaurant, but a tax refund is used for paying bills. As a result of this labelling, there is an additional constraint that dictates spending patterns, and consequently these patterns could seem irrational.[17]

7 *Impatience and Self-control*: While many individuals are fully aware that they need to engage in virtuous behaviours (e.g., saving more, eating healthy food, avoiding procrastination), they often do not act on this knowledge. The dominant paradigm in this research is one of hyperbolic discounting.[18] This paradigm suggests that when people make a choice between a sooner and smaller reward (SS) and a larger and later reward (LL) from a temporal distance, they are aware that the value of LL exceeds that of SS. However, when they move close to SS (either in time or physical distance), they fall into a "lapse zone" that temporarily blinds them to the attractiveness of LL. For instance, most people choose to receive $120 in 53 weeks rather than $100 in 52 weeks; however a significantly smaller number will accept $120

in a week versus $100 now. Note that SS and LL are metaphors of many choices we make – the choice between consuming a $5 cappuccino today (SS) or padding the retirement fund with an extra amount (LL); or the choice between eating an unhealthy dessert (SS) today versus enjoying a healthier life in old age (LL). A related body of research is the work on distributed choice, situations in which many small decisions that are spread out over time aggregate to result in a consequence.[19] For instance, an individual cigarette (or unhealthy treat) will likely not cause any significant harm to one's health, but a lifetime of smoking (or overeating) will. Likewise, spending in moderation and on occasion is not harmful, but a habit of doing so can be disastrous.

One remarkable feature of these insights is that these tendencies are seen almost universally all around the globe. People from affluent parts of the world are as loss averse as those from poorer parts, and universally all consumers tend to be myopic, to demonstrate mental accounting, to fall prey to context effects, to be overwhelmed by information complexity, and to be poor evaluators of value. However, there are differences of degree. Research shows that the magnitude of these behavioural biases increases as slackness in cognitive resources and lack of attention go up. These conditions can be particularly true for consumers among the poorest of the poor. Ram Charan, a farmer who participated in one of my studies in rural India, works on three jobs with irregular pay schedules to provide for his family of three children and two elderly parents. He is perpetually busy and does not have the cognitive capacity to devote to making complex decisions. A flower seller in Chennai – a participant in research conducted by Eldar Shafir and Sendhil Mullainathan – lives her economic life one day at a time and does not have a very good conceptual grasp of the notion of "long term." The decision biases and phenomena outlined earlier create suboptimalities for the most sophisticated consumers in Western societies. But for the financially and temporally constrained farmer and flower seller, the magnitude of these biases and their resulting consequences could be significantly larger.

The Psychology of Adoption and Usage

The insights from behavioural economics help us understand why people do not adopt potentially path-breaking innovations. In some cases, people are simply lazy, and the status quo bias prompts them to stay away from making any changes. In other instances, the innovation is complex, and consumers may lack the cognitive resources to value its benefits. Yet, as John Gourville articulates in a *Harvard Business Review* article, two factors best explain the lack of adoption – gain-loss asymmetries, and the deviation from the status quo.

The adoption of an innovation typically involves a gain and a loss.[20] The consumer needs to give up an existing manner of reaching a goal in exchange for a new way of reaching the same goal. Adopting an electric car in favour of a traditional fossil-fuel powered vehicle involves a loss of the "easy refuelling" feature for the gain of a cleaner environment. Choosing to shop for groceries on Webvan rather than at the traditional grocery store entails the loss of the ability to handpick fresh produce and meat for the gain of convenience. And the adoption of mobile money (like M-Pesa) involves giving up the metering ability of cash and the element of personal control for the gain in convenience and larger access. In each of these cases, unless the gain is significantly larger than the loss, consumers are unlikely to adopt. Furthermore, it is important not only for the gain to be large but for the increased gain to be effectively communicated and compellingly demonstrated.

A second factor that inhibits the adoption of radically new innovations is the resulting behavioural change that is required of the consumer. Consider the example of electric cars. Consumers today have become attuned to a certain pattern of behaviour when they drive. In particular, they fill up with fuel when convenient and continue to drive till the level of fuel in the tank reaches a low level. At that time, they look around for a filling station, refill, and drive on. The electric car requires a fundamentally different pattern of behaviour: consumers need the discipline to charge their cars overnight because they do not have easy access to charging stations as they drive around during the day. In the end, the degree of behaviour change is large enough that consumers have not embraced the innovation as wholeheartedly as the "better mousetrap" idea would suggest.

Could the proponents of the electric car have learned from this behavioural analysis and done something differently? Perhaps, yes. Perhaps they could have considered a model in which consumers do not charge their cars but instead charge a bank of batteries that could be easily unloaded from and loaded into the car. And perhaps there could have been a network of charged battery distributors all over the city. Now a consumer using an electric car would have behaviourally mimicked a consumer using a petrol car, pulling into a battery distributor when the charge is low and switching their discharged batteries for a set of fully charged batteries for a fee.

A second set of examples where the degree of behaviour change inhibits the adoption of new ideas comes from my own research in the fields of rural India. In one case, farmers were being encouraged to adopt techniques that would maximize the yield of their crops. To achieve this, farmers were told that they needed to plant seeds at prescribed intervals – any closer and the roots of adjacent plants would interfere with each other, any farther apart and scarce land would be unutilized. In the educational workshops, farmers understood the need to follow this advice and fully planned to plant according to the prescribed guidelines. Yet, after painstakingly planting a couple of rows, farmers would typically get frustrated with the work involved and resort to what they normally did – scatter seeds over the plot. One quick solution (in the nature of what is called a *jugaad* solution) was to present the farmers with a seeding sheet; a large sheet of plastic with holes drilled in it at the prescribed distance. Now the farmers could continue their habit of scattering seeds on the sheet and driving a tractor over the sheet to plant them; only now the seeds would get planted with the prescribed pattern.

In a similar vein, the adoption of financial literacy solutions in the cash economy of rural India presented an enigma. In work with Amar Cheema, we taught agricultural and construction labourers how to create a budget and the basic principles of household finances.[21] A banker also helped them with a crude financial plan and recommended savings targets. However, even though the labourers agreed with the need and had the means to save, the behavioural change needed to maintain spending records and balance budgets proved too much and savings rates never did go up.

In order to address the savings challenge, we used a principle from mental accounting called earmarking: the labelling of money for a specific use as a tactic to solve the last mile savings problem. Earmarking is conceptually similar to budgeting as described by Heath and Soll, among others.[22] For example, in interviews we conducted in North America to understand household money management practices, several respondents used the term "earmarking" for the practice of allocating money towards various categories of purchases, using a desktop computer application. However, earmarking often takes on a more specific form; one in which the earmarked money is kept distinct from other monies either through physical segregation or through other forms of categorization (e.g., a separate bank account). Prior research suggests that the act of earmarking makes the money more "sticky" towards the particular spending goal it was designated for.

Participating households in this study were given their cash salaries in two separate parts: (a) their earmarked savings, and (b) the rest of the wage. Our results showed that the act of earmarking significantly increased savings rates. We also found that this effect could be strengthened by putting a photograph of the children on top of each earmarked envelope and sealing it. When the envelopes had photographs (rather than a plain white surface), the likelihood that the earmarked savings envelopes would be opened was reduced dramatically. These results show that simple psychological interventions that reinforce the process of behavioural change can greatly facilitate the adoption of new ideas and innovations. Small transaction costs can trip up the best intentions; hence, products and interventions that enable/allow the individual to perform the desired tasks with minimal transaction costs will increase the chance that they can execute their plans. These products could be as simple as an envelope or a piggy-bank, or as complex as an online planner. In another research example, we used budgeting boards with colour-coded zones to allow farmers to do the budgeting tasks better. Rather than thinking about their surplus income and what to do with it, they now simply follow the colour coding on the boards.[23]

In sum, the non-adoption of innovations typically results from a large empathy gap between the innovators and the consumers. Innovators are – by definition – among the self-selected few who are convinced that the product works, have thought about the precise need that their product addresses, and are dissatisfied with the existing offerings in the marketplace. Consumers have a different perspective. They are sceptical about the innovation and they often do not see the need for it. I conclude this chapter with a set of prescriptions for how an innovator might set out to tackle these challenges.

Finally, I would like to emphasize a point that many innovators and marketers often miss: adoption is only meaningful if the adopters of the product actually use the product and continue to reuse it. The decision to use an adopted product is complex and multifaceted, but again has roots in the insights from behavioural economics. In particular, mental accounting dictates that when people prepay for a product or a consumption opportunity, the only way they can satisfactorily close their mental account "in the black" is by consuming the product. Therefore, making the cost of a consumption opportunity salient can boost consumption. John Gourville and I have demonstrated this principle across several studies with health club patrons and members of a theatre festival.[24] We found that when payment was made salient (e.g., when the payment had just been made, when payment was done by cash or check rather than with a credit card, and when the transaction format allowed for the coupling of the payment with the consumption opportunity), consumption rates were high compared to situations in which the payment was not very salient. Likewise, research on self-perception suggests that the degree to which consumers are invested in a particular project can signal their commitment to the project. Both lines of thinking suggest that paying for medication or advice (rather than receiving it free, as typically happens) is likely to make individuals more committed to taking that medication or using that advice.

More generally, innovators need to understand that their marketing efforts should not end when the innovation is purchased – usage, repeat purchase, and continued usage all need to be included among the defined end goals of the marketing effort.

What Does All This Mean for the Innovator?

I have argued in this chapter that consumers – especially those in the Global South – will not necessarily beat a path to the door of the innovator who has built the best mousetrap. I have painted the picture of a consumer who is cognitively constrained and emotionally driven, a consumer who strives for simplicity in information and ease of use and who relies heavily on the status quo and defaults. From an economic perspective, this consumer is irrational – but as Ariely and others have argued, the good news is that she is not erratically but rather predictably irrational.[25] An innovator who internalizes all of these behavioural stories and embeds them in the design of the innovation has produced what I would call a "behaviourally informed innovation."

What does all of this mean for the innovator? In the next few paragraphs, I outline several prescriptions for the innovator who seeks to be behaviourally informed.

Articulate the Value Proposition: A *value proposition* is simply a statement that articulates the nature of the promised value to be delivered. Marketing textbooks and gurus have repeatedly advised us that the most effective value proposition statements are written in consumer language, and describe the value as experienced by the consumer. In particular, value proposition statements should focus not on the differentiating attributes of the product (i.e., not on why this mousetrap is better than others) but on the resulting benefit for the consumer.

In my book co-authored with Sara N-Marandi, we present a taxonomy of value.[26] On one dimension, value could be either economic or experiential. An innovation creates economic value if it can perform a task more efficiently or effectively, resulting in a cost saving or a revenue increase – in effect, if it can influence the customer's financial bottom line. The volume-based "production processes" at the Aravind Eye Hospital or the Narayan cardiac hospital in India are examples of economic value creation. At the other end of the spectrum is experiential value – the value the customer gets because they enjoy the experience of using the product. They may enjoy either the consumption itself, or they may get value if the innovation allows them to achieve an aspiration.

When innovations deliver economic value, it is tempting to focus on the cost savings created and ignore the aspirations and the experiences of the consumer. The Tata Nano, an affordable, no-frills car, was designed to appeal to the many Indian consumers who drive motorcycles. The cost of manufacturing the vehicle was brought down by eliminating many non-essential features, and the car was marketed with affordability as the key value proposition. Likewise, the Garib Rath is a no-frills air-conditioned train launched by Indian Railways for passengers who cannot afford normal fares. Unfortunately, the term "Garib Rath" literally translated to the "Chariot of the Poor." Both these introductions struggled because they failed to take into account the aspirations of the target consumer. Low-income consumers did not work hard and save money just to buy a car or take a train for the poor; their aspirations were to join the middle class.

A second manner of classifying value has to do with the locus of the value. An innovation like high-definition TV (HDTV) improves the quality of the consumption experience itself – the manner in which the target product is consumed. For example, HDTV gives a better viewing experience; fully reclining beds in a plane improve the level of comfort in a flight; and the newest cell phones give a better call quality. We refer to these as value with an internal locus. The term "internal" refers to the fact that the value creation occurs when the product is used. In contrast, innovations with an external locus of value are those in which the customers gain utility not through the consumption experience itself, but through its implications for other activities they perform. DVRs do not provide better quality television viewing on their own, but they do allow customers greater flexibility in scheduling their time. And while a handheld PDA device such as a Blackberry or iPhone does not necessarily improve call quality or make it easier to send e-mails, it does allow customers to utilize their time more effectively. Managers also report that external locus innovations were typically much more sustainable in the long run. These innovations last longer, and the rates of customer acceptability increase with time. A value proposition with an external locus also typically appeals to agents other than the end user, allowing for creative revenue models to be used to make the innovation an economic success.

Consider a recent innovation in India: the Aakash tablet computer. The Aakash is a low-cost Android-based tablet computer with a seven-inch touch screen and a USB port, and is designed to operate on low bandwidth networks. Interestingly, the Aakash tablet is not merely a tablet computer but a conduit through which various interactive contents could reach the vast hinterland of India. Education, including public health education, financial information, weather and agricultural information, and market information are all examples of the value that the Aakash tablet can bring to its users. In doing so, Aakash can also create value for agencies interested in disseminating education and promoting effective agricultural practices. It is easy to foresee complex revenue models for the Aakash tablet, with the end user paying only a subsidized price for the tablet and with other agencies that stand to gain from its widespread penetration providing larger chunks of revenue.

Choice Architecture – Nudging the Consumer to Make the Right Choice: Perhaps one of the major ideas emanating from the field of behavioural economics is the notion of choice architecture.[27] We know that choices change as the context in which they are made changes; could we look at the converse and engineer contexts to nudge consumers towards making a particular choice?

Consider the example of organ donation from earlier in the chapter. Different European countries had adopted different defaults without any strategic reason. In many cases the defaults came from societal norms or were simply borrowed from other regimes. However, the government of Wales is now in the process of converting their opt-in organ donation system (where the default is to not donate) to an opt-out system.[28] This is a classic example of choice architecture with the goal of encouraging more people to become organ donors. Similarly, automatic enrolment in savings plans has been used to encourage more people to save for retirement. Choice architecture essentially simplifies the consumer's task and efficiently conveys the information needed to make the right choice.

The biggest impact of choice architecture is in helping consumers manage the gap between intention and action that we referred to earlier. It can help by getting people to (for example) open bank accounts, buy new products, sign up for services, or get access to health care. However, it is important to note that these are only the first stages of successful consumer engagement. Choice architecture needs to be followed by interventions that continuously engage the user – through, for example, making ongoing savings deposits, repeatedly using products and services, and regularly visiting health-care facilities.

Integrate the Innovation into Existing Ecosystems and Behaviours: The most compelling innovations add value above and beyond the benefits gained just by using the product. However, for there to be an external locus of value (as discussed earlier), the innovation must not require any significant change in behaviour. The M-Pesa is perhaps the most advanced mobile payment system anywhere in the world, and one of the cornerstones of its success is the fact that it was piggy-backed onto existing high rates of mobile phone ownership and use in Kenya. The added benefits of adopting and using M-Pesa were obvious to end users, and the additional costs were negligible since most people already carried a mobile phone. Another example of successful integration into an existing behavioural pattern is Sprinkles. Sprinkles is an innovative way of providing supplements to address vitamin and mineral deficiencies. These micronutrients are sold in powder form and can be easily added to home-cooked meals. The integration occurs through the packaging – the micronutrients are sold in individual "serving size" sachets. Consumers in the Global South are used to purchasing sachet-size packages of shampoos, detergents, snacks, and even toothpaste. Distribution through a sachet fits the mental accounting of daily labourers whose economic lives are a succession of single days. For households used to sachet purchasing, Sprinkles was easy to adopt – once consumers were sold on the need for the nutrients – and the integration into existing behaviours gave consumers the right nudge to adopt.

Develop Innovations from the Bottom Up: Given that human behaviour is complex, context dependent, and subject to social, cultural, and national nuances, it seems obvious that the best innovations are those that are developed from the towns and fields and the communities in which they will eventually be used. Elsewhere in this book, Anita McGahan and her collaborators refer to this style of innovation as embedded innovation and delve into its nature in depth. For now, I will simply underscore the importance of understanding the context before any products or services are designed. The best way of reducing the empathy gap between the innovator and the consumer is for the innovator to live the life of a consumer, identify unmet needs, and develop solutions based on a rich understanding of consumer behaviour. Ethnography is a particularly powerful tool to use in the embedded style of innovation.

THE IDEA IN BRIEF

Innovations often fail because innovators have a flawed understanding of the psychology of the end user. Consumers construct value as a function of the context and are not necessarily driven purely by rational considerations.

IMPLICATIONS

1 Articulate your intended value proposition before you produce and distribute.
2 Use choice architecture to nudge the consumer to purchase and to consume.
3 Integrate the innovation into existing ecosystems and behaviours.

FOOD FOR THOUGHT

The more context dependent an innovation is, the more valuable it is for the local consumer, yet the more challenging it will be to scale up. What is the optimal level of "contextualization" for balancing these dual considerations?

REFERENCES

1 Yule, S.S.B., & Keane, M.S. (1891). *Borrowings*. San Francisco, CA: Murdock.
2 Schneider, J., & Hall, J. (2011). "Why most product launches fail." *Harvard Business Review* (April).
3 Soman, D., Kumar, V., Metcalfe, M., & Wong, J. (2012). "Beyond great ideas: A framework for going global with local innovations." *Rotman Magazine* (Fall): 50–5.

4 Thaler, R.H., & Sunstein, C.R. (2008). *Nudge: Improving decisions about health, wealth, & happiness*. New Haven, CT: Yale University Press; and Mullainathan, S. (2009). *Solving social problems with a nudge*. Presentation given at the TED conference in India (7 November). Retrieved 10 March 2010 from http://www.youtube.com/watch?v=XBJQENjZJaA.

5 Ratner, R.R., Soman, D., Zauberman, G., Ariely, D., Anand Keller, P., Carmon, Z., et al. (2008). "How behavioral decision research can enhance consumer welfare: From freedom of choice to paternalistic interventions." *Marketing Letters* 19 (3–4) (December): 383–97; and Soman, D., Xu, J., & Cheema, A. (2010). "Decision points: A theory emerges." *Rotman Magazine* (Winter): 64–8.

6 Bertrand, M., Karlan, D.S., Mullainathan, S., Shafir, E., & Zinman, J. (2005). *What's psychology worth? A field experiment in the consumer credit market*. Discussion paper no. 918, Economic Growth Center, Yale University, New Haven, CT.

7 Brown, Louise. (2011). "Canada Learning Bond helps low-income families." *Toronto Star*, 26 June. Retrieved 15 September 2012 from http://www.thestar.com/news/article/1015294--psst-free-money-for-higher-learning-is-anyone-there; redirected to: http://www.thestar.com/life/parent/2011/06/26/canada_learning_bond_helps_lowincome_families.html.

8 Johnson, E., & Goldstein, D. (2003). "Do defaults save lives?" *Science* 32 (5649) (21 November): 1338–9.

9 Ariely, D., Loewenstein, G., & Prelec, D. (2006). "Tom Sawyer and the construction of value." *Journal of Economic Behavior and Organization* 60: 1–10.

10 Kahneman, D., & Tversky, A. (1979). "Prospect theory: An analysis of decision under risk." *Econometrica* XLVII : 263–91.

11 Simonson, Itamar. (1989). "Choice based on reasons: The case of attraction and compromise effects." *Journal of Consumer Research* 16 (2) (September): 158–74.

12 See Soman, Dilip. (2010). "Option overload: How to deal with choice complexity." *Rotman Magazine* (Fall): 43–7, for a review.

13 Huberman, G., Iyengar, S.S., & Jiang W. (2007). "Defined contribution pension plans: Determinants of participation & contribution rates." *Journal of Financial Services Research* 31 (1): 1–32.

14 The term was originally coined by Richard Thaler. See Thaler, R. (1985). "Mental accounting & consumer choice." *Marketing Science* 4: 199–214.

15 Soman, D., & Ahn, H.-K. (2011). "Mental accounting & individual welfare." In G. Keren (Ed.), *Perspectives on framing*, 65–92. New York: Psychology Press/Taylor & Francis.

16 See Zelizer, V.A. (1994). "The creation of domestic currencies." *American Economic Review* 84 (2) (May): 138–42; and Zelizer, V.A. (1997). *The social meaning of money: Pin money, paychecks, poor relief, and other currencies*. Princeton, NJ: Princeton University Press.

17 See O'Curry, S. (2000). "Income source effects." DePaul University, Working Paper; and McGraw, P., Tetlock, P.E., & Kristel, O. (2003). "The limits of fungibility: Relational schemata and the value of things." *Journal of Consumer Research* 30 (2): 219–29.

18 See Ainslie, G., & Haslam, N. (1992). "Self-control," In G. Loewenstein & J. Elster (Eds), *Choice over time*, 177–209. New York: Sage. See also Hoch, S.J., & Loewenstein, G.F. (1991). "Time-inconsistent preferences & consumer self-control." *Journal of Consumer Research* 17: 492–507 for a discussion on self-control strategies.

19 Herrnstein, R.J., & Prelec, D. (1991). "Melioration: A theory of distributed choice." *Journal of Economic Perspectives* 5 (3): 137–56.

20 Gourville, John. (2006). "Eager sellers and stony buyers: Understanding the psychology of new product adoption." *Harvard Business Review* (June).

21 Soman, D., & Cheema, A. (2011). "Earmarking and partitioning: Increasing saving by low-income households." *Journal of Marketing Research* 48 (Special): S14–S22.

22 See Heath, C., & Soll, J.B. (1996). "Mental budgeting & consumer decisions." *Journal of Consumer Research* 23: 40–52, for an excellent description of the psychology of budgeting. See also Thaler, R.H. (1999). "Mental accounting matters." *Journal of Behavioral Decision Making* 12: 183–206.

23 See Soman, Xu, & Cheema. (2010), "Decision points: A theory emerges."

24 Gourville, J., & Soman, D. (2002). "Pricing and the psychology of consumption." *Harvard Business Review* (September): 90–6.

25 Ariely, D. (2008). *Predictably irrational*. New York: Harper Collins.

26 Soman, D., & N-Marandi, S. (2009). *Managing customer value: One stage at a time*. Singapore: World Scientific Publishing.

27 Thaler & Sunstein (2008), *Nudge*.

28 Retrieved 30 September 2012 from http://www.guardian.co.uk/society/2012/jun/18/wales-organ-donor-scheme-opt-out.

3

Appropriate Technologies for the Global South

YU-LING CHENG
BEVERLY BRADLEY

Introduction

The rapid pace of technological innovation over the past few decades in sectors ranging from telecommunications to health care has been breathtaking. These innovations have led to tremendous improvements in our standard of living. We are healthier, we live longer, we are more productive, and we enjoy a broader range of social, cultural, educational, entertainment, and recreational options than ever before. However, there is large disparity in the distribution of the benefits of technological innovations across varying economic sectors of the world population. For example, life expectancy in the wealthiest countries has been increasing over time, likely as a result of improved health-care technologies. In contrast, the income needed to achieve fractional levels of health or survival among adults in low-income countries has been increasing over the past five decades[1] (that is, it is getting more expensive for the poor adults of the world to be healthy). Simple necessities such as clean drinking water, basic sanitation, and sufficient food supply that are provided by technologies taken for granted in the developed world remain inaccessible to billions of people. The root causes of inequity in access to and benefits from technology are complex, but a key factor is that innovations conceived and created in the developed world without reference to circumstances in the Global South often fail to be implemented successfully.

There are many examples of technologies that have not produced the desired benefits. Martin Fisher, founder of KickStart, has criticized the ineffectiveness of giving inappropriate equipment as a form of aid: "The tragedy ... throughout Africa is that it is littered with broken down water systems and farm equipment."[2] A prime example is the PlayPump: the concept involves harnessing energy from children as they play on carousels to pump water from underground aquifers, thus saving women from the drudgery of fetching or pumping water. Designed by South Africans Ronnie Styver and Trevor Field, the somewhat whimsical idea captured the attention of donors and international agencies, and by 2009 more than 1,000 PlayPumps had been installed throughout Africa, sometimes in conjunction with the removal of pre-existing wells or pumps. However, the reality is that children do not play long enough to pump enough water for the needs of the communities, and adult women do not use such pumps because they feel it is undignified to play on a carousel. Mixed success was seen in the pilot countries, and many PlayPumps now sit idle while clean water supplies for communities have been compromised. In March 2010, PlayPumps International, the not-for-profit established to disseminate PlayPumps throughout Africa, closed its doors and donated its inventory to Water For People, an organization now working to address the challenges encountered with the PlayPump through innovations in functionality and safety in order to ensure that the technology is used appropriately.

Health-care technologies also suffer from inappropriateness. Figure 3.1 shows discarded walkers piled outside the Royal Victoria Hospital in The Gambia. The walkers were likely gifts from well-meaning donors, but are unusable given the road conditions in The Gambia. Perry and Malkin have systematically surveyed the use of medical equipment in sixteen developing nations and found a significant fraction (about 40 per cent) to be in disuse and disrepair.[3] Cost, lack of skilled staff to maintain and operate equipment, lack of funds to purchase spare parts or consumables, and irrelevance in the local context are among the reasons that equipment and technologies have not been used effectively and thus cannot benefit the target communities.[4] These conditions also call into question the effectiveness of equipment donations to hospitals in developing countries.

Figure 3.1: Discarded walkers outside the Royal Victoria Hospital, The Gambia, 2009. (Photograph courtesy of David Luong)

In this chapter, we survey the ways in which technological innovations are being made more appropriate and therefore more useful in the Global South. Schumacher's *Small Is Beautiful*[5] launched an ideological movement that focused on small and simple technologies that have sometimes been equated with appropriate technologies. We take a broader definition of appropriate technology – that is, if a technology is used for its intended purpose by the intended target users, then it is appropriate for that setting. Our survey begins with a discussion of how existing technologies can be made more appropriate, through the judicious selection of the right commercially available technologies, through providing the support ecosystem to make the operation and maintenance of existing technologies more feasible, or through driving down the cost to make the technologies more affordable. We then highlight innovations in appropriate technologies, categorized into two major themes: appropriateness through user acceptability ("behaviourally informed innovations,"[6] as introduced by Soman in chapter 2); and appropriateness through engineering and design (new cutting-edge technologies based on novel engineering design and in-depth analysis). We highlight strategies such as increasing cultural congruence and designing technically innovative solutions as examples of useful approaches to innovating for the other 90 per cent. We then take a look at who the innovators of appropriate technology actually are. Finally, we discuss the innovation process and ways of making innovation more efficient and scalable for the greatest global impact.

Making Existing Technologies Appropriate

In spite of many failures, some technologies have been successfully implemented. Apart from designing new innovations that are appropriate for developing regions, an alternative approach to broadening the benefits of technology is to increase the rate of successful implementation of existing technologies – that is, to find ways to make existing technologies more appropriate. Aside from social and cultural issues, mismatches between a technology and its intended setting may lie in the technology itself, in the support ecosystem, or simply in the cost; efforts to overcome each of these types of mismatch are progressing.

Choosing the Right Commercially Available Technologies

It is so obvious that it shouldn't have to be said, but not all technologies are suitable for all settings. A farm tractor is an inappropriate vehicle for residents in downtown Toronto; a furnace or heater is inappropriate in tropical settings. Similarly, walkers designed for places with well-paved sidewalks are inappropriate where dirt roads are the norm, and hospital equipment such as MRI machines that depend on stable power delivery for operation, cooling, or temperature control are not appropriate for settings where power is unreliable or in scarce supply.

Unfortunately, the "suitability" issue does not seem to be commonly recognized. Most health technology is produced by companies from high-income countries, and, too often, well-intentioned donations of such equipment to resource-poor countries are inappropriate for the context and needs of the recipient facilities. Supporting better equipment donation practices is one step towards increasing the amount of functional and effective technology in developing countries.[7]

In some cases, the mismatch is at a more detailed technical level, and is less obvious to users who lack the required technical expertise. One such example involved oxygen concentrators donated to a hospital in The Gambia. The concentrators had the wrong voltages and frequencies for the hospital power source, but the hospital did not have the technical expertise to evaluate the equipment. Not surprisingly, the concentrators broke as a result of overheating shortly after installation.[8]

Careful evaluation of equipment for performance characteristics in the intended setting would lead to a much higher rate of successful use. Peel and colleagues selected eleven off-the-shelf oxygen concentrators from seven manufacturers that have voltage and frequency ranges appropriate for a broad geographical reach, then characterized and ranked these models by cost, power consumption, oxygen flow rate, operating temperature, operating range of humidity and altitude, warranty period, and cost of replacement parts. It was concluded that only six of the eleven models met the minimum criteria for appropriateness in a tropical setting. One manufacturer stood out among the rest, offering four models that ranked the highest relative to all surveyed models according to the selected criteria.[9] An assessment of oxygen concentrators in Malawi and Mongolia also showed significant variation in performance among the different models of concentrators installed in these countries;[10] notably, both units by the manufacturer selected by Peel were being successfully used.

In addition to choosing appropriate devices, those responsible for choosing equipment can sometimes adapt the operating context or the system surrounding a device to improve appropriateness. For example, Bradley and colleagues have explored the use of batteries as a backup power supply for oxygen concentrator machines in contexts where grid power is intermittent and unreliable.[11] They have also explored the cost-effectiveness of other oxygen system configurations, including options that store oxygen instead of energy.[12] In general, batteries and other alternative power sources such as solar panels are being used to operate several different medical technologies, including vaccine refrigerators, laboratory microscopes, and diagnostic technologies. Careful analysis of the available options and the target context when choosing appropriate alternative power options or other system-supporting mechanisms is another way to make it possible for existing technologies to function successfully in settings that perhaps were not their intended environment.

Rigorous evaluation and selection procedures for off-the-shelf technologies can be applied to any technology if the appropriate expertise exists within either donor or recipient organizations. Emerging organizations (referred to as medical surplus recovery organizations) such as Humatem and the Catholic Health Association are focused on developing best practices in equipment donation and assessment/evaluation methodologies to ensure a higher success rate of donations. The World Health Organization has also published guidelines for equipment donation.[13] Examples of criteria set out by these organizations include the following: suitability for the skill levels of the available operators and maintenance personnel; compatibility with existing utilities and energy supplies; suitability to the local climate, geography, and conditions; ability to be run economically with local resources; availability of instructions and manuals in the appropriate language(s); and the existence of a supply channel for equipment-related supplies (e.g., consumables). Similar assessment methodologies and criteria can and should be applied to the acquisition of new commercially available equipment or even the design of equipment.[14]

Providing the Support Ecosystem to Make
Existing Technologies Appropriate

A second and extremely important factor that makes some technologies inappropriate is the lack of available skilled labour to operate and maintain a device or piece of equipment. This happens at varying levels of technological complexity. Technologies intended for home use need to be suitable for the skill levels of the general population, while hospital equipment should be suited to the skill levels of hospital technicians or health-care workers.

Unlike mismatches in technical specifications, appropriateness in the skills dimension is relative. New technologies may be designed to match existing skill levels; or, alternatively, training may be provided to upgrade skills so maintenance can be performed on existing technologies. Such training would not be practical for technologies meant for use by the general population, but there are growing efforts to provide training to upgrade skill levels for maintaining and operating specialized equipment that is used in hospitals. Curriculum and programs for biomedical engineering technologists or assistant technicians in Zambia,[15] Rwanda,[16] Ethiopia,[17] Uganda,[18] and Nepal[19] were reported at a recent conference. Malkin and colleagues conducted a controlled study showing that the provision of training for technologists improves the effective use of hospital equipment.[20]

An even more basic issue than the availability of trained technicians is the need for the tools required for maintenance. Adjabu and colleagues report that supplying even simple tools, such as screwdrivers and wrenches, can make a crucial difference in keeping a piece of equipment operational.[21]

Making Existing Technologies Cheaper

Another way to make existing technologies more accessible is to drive down the cost through technological adaptations (as was done with the more affordable vehicles produced by Tata and Mobius Motors). Some technologies, such as cell phones, can be manufactured much more cheaply today as a result of the natural progression of technological advancement and the use of lower cost/lower quality parts. As well, forgoing the latest advances that attract early adopters (e.g., better touch screens, faster operating systems) has enabled India and China to produce even more affordable models. The Aakash tablet by DataWind, which will be discussed later in the chapter, is an example of an innovation focused on driving down cost.

Other efforts aim to reduce the cost of a technology to the end user through subsidized donation schemes. For example, in an effort to increase safe surgical practices in low-resource countries, the not-for-profit organization LifeBox is offering pulse oximeters accompanied with training materials to health facilities in need for $250 (U.S.), or at no cost if there is a willing donor to cover the cost. A recent National Health Service (NHS) market survey of pulse oximeters lists the cost of comparable handheld units at between $230 (U.S.) and $9,280 (U.S.),[22] the majority of which were well over $250 (U.S.).[23]

Innovations in Appropriate Technologies

Sometimes the differences between the needs, problems, constraints, and contexts of developed and developing regions are so great that off-the-shelf solutions do not exist. For these challenges, technologies need to be developed de novo. Factors that must be considered include cost structure, social/cultural acceptability, and technical functionality. In surveying this space, we found a spectrum of technical approaches towards developing appropriate technologies, ranging from simple, low-technology solutions to cutting-edge scientific solutions.

We have categorized these approaches along two dimensions: innovations that are appropriate because of high user acceptability, and innovations that focus on technological advances. There are many

examples of simple technical or conceptual innovations that are inge-
nious in the way they are applied to match user needs. Cutting-edge
technological advances can be equally appropriate if user acceptability
factors are considered as part of the development process.

Innovation for High User Acceptability

One way to increase user acceptability is to increase cultural acceptability by minimizing or avoiding the need to change behaviours that are
deeply entrenched in cultural norms. Cultural acceptability is an important factor in the sustainable adoption of new technologies. This factor sometimes skews technologies towards the simple approaches. Rita
Colwell headed a team that studied the effectiveness of using multiple
layers of used sari cloths for filtering cholera bacteria on plankton from
drinking water.[24] Single layers of sari cloth are routinely used in Bangladesh communities to remove dirt from water, and using multiple layers
did not significantly change the customary way of filtering water. In
their study, a 48 per cent reduction in cholera cases among multi-layer
filter users was observed. The minimal change in customary behaviour
was well accepted, and the community continued to practice multi-
layer filtration sixteen months after its introduction.[25]

The ultimate in cultural acceptability comes with technologies that
are completely transparent to the user. The use of double-fortified salt
and Ultra-Rice are two approaches of this type. Deficiencies in essential
micronutrients can hinder mental and physical development. For people with poor diets, micronutrient fortification is a strategy that can
provide essential micronutrients inexpensively.

Salt is an ideal carrier for micronutrients because it is nearly universally used, and the amount of salt consumed is largely independent of
diet, so overdosing is not a risk. Iodized salt has been widely available in
the United States since the 1920s. Although global coverage is still not
universal, iodized salt is available in many parts of the world. The addition of other micronutrients to iodized salt would help supplement poor
diets. Fortifying iodized salt with iron requires the encapsulation of iron
in a protective coating to act as a barrier to prevent iron-iodine interactions, and it took several years of research to develop stable formula-
tions.[26] The end product, however, is a double-fortified salt that, to the
consumer, looks and tastes like normal salt or iodized salt; and no change
in behaviour is required. Field studies have shown marked reductions in
iodine and iron deficiencies in study populations; for example, a trial in

Moroccan school children showed significantly improved urinary iodine concentrations, and the prevalence of iron deficiency anaemia decreased from 35 per cent at baseline to 8 per cent after just forty weeks.[27]

Ultra-Rice similarly does not require changes in user behaviour. It is made of rice flour fortified with a range of essential minerals and vitamins and formulated to look like rice grains as well as to be stable under rice preparation conditions. Ultra-Rice can then be mixed with normal rice grains. For consumers, the process of preparing and consuming Ultra-Rice is no different from that for regular rice; no behaviour change is required.[28]

All three of these examples, the sari cloth filter, double-fortified salt, and Ultra-Rice, are innovations that avoid the common assumption (or misconception), referred to in the earlier chapter by Soman, that the user will assess and evaluate value in the technology and adopt it rationally.[29] Indeed, when it comes to appropriate technologies, one way to tackle the "last mile" problem is to seamlessly embed the technology into normal cultural or social practices so that little or no behavioural change by the end user is required.

A second approach to increasing user acceptability, as prescribed in chapter 2, is to introduce a value proposition[30] (i.e., make technologies that are valuable to consumers). As difficult as it is to modify behaviour, there are many examples of technology adoption that have required behaviour change, demonstrating that consumers, including financially and temporally constrained consumers, are willing to modify behaviour if they see value in the technology.

For the poorest of the poor, extreme affordability is a requirement that skews solutions towards the simple and low-technology end of the spectrum. The small-scale low-technology approach is in some ways the ideological descendant of the movement launched in 1973 with the publication of Schumacher's influential book *Small Is Beautiful*.[31] Consistent with this ideology, KickStart and International Development Enterprise (IDE) are two prominent organizations that are developing and selling small-scale, low-cost, easy-to-maintain farm equipment such as treadle pumps and low-drip irrigation piping to farmers who earn $1 a day. Paul Polak, the founder of IDE, argues that poor farmers should be treated like any other consumers who will be motivated to purchase and adopt products if they can afford them and if they see value in them. In Polak's view, the most effective way to test the usefulness of products and equipment for the poor is to sell it: *"If you can't sell it, don't make it."*[32] The simple products developed and sold or provided by IDE and

KickStart that are effectively lifting $1-a-day farmers out of poverty are examples of technologies that bring economic value[33] to their users.

Simple technologies intended to bring experiential value[34] to users often do not require many years and large research budgets to develop, and have therefore attracted faculty and students in engineering and business design courses. Amy Smith of the Massachusetts Institute of Technology's (MIT) D-Lab has been spearheading university-level courses on design for extreme affordability. Projects in these courses have led to very clever and useful innovations. One example is low-emission charcoal briquettes made from agricultural waste that minimize particle emissions and the detrimental health effects of indoor cooking. A second example is a hand-powered walnut cracker. A similar course recently introduced at the University of Toronto has resulted in a simple squat-assistive device that can be mass produced for about $1 per unit designed to help physically weaker people such as seniors use a squat toilet. Students at Stanford's D.School developed the Embrace Incubator. This ingeniously simple product for keeping premature babies warm is essentially a sleeping bag insulated with a phase-change material that stores or releases heat while maintaining the temperature at 37°C. The idea requires some understanding of materials and thermodynamics but is well within the capabilities of undergraduate engineering students. The product serves the same function as sophisticated Western-style incubators at less than 1 per cent of the cost.

Going beyond undergraduate-level engineering design and analysis, Jan Andrysek of the Bloorview Research Institute at the University of Toronto has used sophisticated biomechanics analysis and high-quality but low-cost thermoplastics to develop the LC Knee – a $50 prosthetic knee joint that can be used by amputees in rough terrain.

A number of great partnerships between academic institutions and non-academic organizations have also been formed to tackle global challenges with simple technologies. An elegantly simple device developed by the Division of Global Health and Human Rights at Massachusetts General Hospital (MGH) is a low-cost uterine balloon for stopping postpartum haemorrhage – the single most important cause of maternal deaths worldwide. The MGH Division, in partnership with the Program for Appropriate Technology in Health (PATH), has rolled out the device in South Sudan and Kenya, with early signs of success. More information is available at Ujenzi.org.

In each of these examples, if the potential users – farmers, health-care workers, parents, seniors, or amputees – can see value in greater farm productivity, keeping a premature baby alive, being able to use a squat toilet, or go back to work, and can afford the products, it has been shown that the value proposition will motivate behaviour change, and that such products have a good chance of being adopted.

Computers and cell phones are perhaps the best known examples of products that motivate behaviour change because of their perceived value in terms of access to information, knowledge, financial systems, and so on. Cell phones have penetrated nearly every corner of life in the developing world: for example, many farmers use cell phones to find markets where they can sell their produce for the highest price. M-Pesa and other mobile-phone-based money transfer and micro-financing services are now available to millions of people in developing countries. Cell phones are also able to check for counterfeit drugs; GlaxoSmithKline (GSK) has developed a short message service (SMS) text-based service called *Hakikisha dawa* to enhance patient safety by allowing people to check the authenticity of GSK-brand drugs.

The pervasiveness of mobile phones has inspired a wide range of applications based on mobile technologies. An MIT D-Lab project has resulted in a cervical cancer diagnostic tool using the camera on a cell phone and an algorithm for image recognition, while a University of Toronto design project has resulted in an iPhone app for diagnosing cataracts.

In October 2011, DataWind, a Montreal-based company led by CEO Suneet Tuli, introduced a $35 tablet computer, called Aakash, with Internet connectivity designed for the Internet system in India, that will make the Internet accessible to a billion people in that country. DataWind designed Aakash with a relentless focus on extreme affordability based on an understanding of the financial realities faced by Indian users and of their high motivation for accessing information and giving their children access to knowledge.

Appropriate Innovation through Technological Advancement

Some innovations motivated by the needs of the Global South have spurred the application of cutting-edge technologies, or the development of new technologies based on sophisticated engineering design and analysis. Two excellent examples are the development of lab-on-chip devices used for point-of-care diagnostics and the project of reinventing the toilet.

Lab-on-chip devices incorporate multiple steps of laboratory test procedures onto a single small "chip" that can be made of a variety of materials, including plastic and glass. Sample processing steps and test reagents incorporated on the chip enable tests that used to require laboratory-scale instruments to be carried out on a small device. The miniaturization makes it possible for diagnostics to be performed at the "point-of-care" – in a doctor's office or in a remote community – rather than requiring samples to be sent to clinical laboratories for testing. The small length scales on these chips translate to much faster assay times, and chips can be designed to minimize human intervention, so that little specialized training is required for conducting the diagnostic tests. Lab-on-chip technologies can potentially revolutionize how diagnostic assays are performed globally. The impact would be particularly significant in settings in developing countries where expensive laboratory instruments (requiring reliable power and temperature control) or large amounts of chemical reagents (requiring refrigeration) would be both prohibitively expensive and a mismatch with available infrastructure.

Lab-on-chip and micro-fluidics technologies are at the forefront of scientific and engineering innovation today. Top research universities around the world are hiring highly trained research faculty in these areas. This cutting-edge technology is also being directed towards the needs of the Global South, with applications focused on diseases that are more prevalent in developing regions – such as HIV, malaria, and tuberculosis. Grand Challenges Canada's (GCC) first call for proposals – on point-of-care diagnostics – attracted a wide range of proposals. From low-cost sample preparation and collection ("patient-to-chip") devices, to handheld biosensors using antigen-specific DNA and Surface Enhanced Raman Spectroscopy, to the reconceptualizion of quantitative real-time polymerase chain reaction (qPCR) for a developing world context, innovators around the world are revolutionizing the disease detection process.

Even though lab-on-chip diagnostics promise to be significantly less expensive than conventional laboratory tests, the cost can still be too high for some applications in developing regions. Paul Yager has been spearheading the drive towards extreme affordability by developing paper-based diagnostics.[35] In an effort to drive down costs as well as encourage cultural acceptance, Dhananjay Denkuri, a GCC grantee, has been developing silk-based lab-on-chip devices in which on-chip patterns of hydrophobic and hydrophilic channels can be formed by traditional weaving of silk threads that are surface-modified to be either hydrophobic or hydrophilic.

The project to reinvent the toilet represents another recent development challenge where cutting-edge technologies are being applied to the needs of the Global South. The Bill and Melinda Gates Foundation (BMGF) launched the "Reinvent the Toilet Challenge" (RTTC) in July 2011 in which researchers from the Centre for Global Engineering (CGEN) at the University of Toronto are participating. Engineering teams from around the world are being challenged to develop technologies to sanitize human waste within twenty-four hours without running water, sewerage infrastructure, or grid power and at a cost of less than five cents per person per day. It is also desirable for the reinvented toilets to be "aspirational," so that people will want them, as well as to be able to capture valuable content from human waste – clean water, fertilizer, or energy.

The need for proper sanitation facilities is enormous, affecting 2.6 billion people in the world – yet it is a need that most in the developed world would not have identified. The specifications are also foreign to Torontonians. The technical aspects of liquid and waste separation and disinfection are challenging enough to develop and integrate, but we also need to consider ease of maintenance, safety, and user motivation. The aspiration and value-capture criteria address considerations of user behaviour modification that are highly relevant to appropriate technologies. For the one billion people in the world who defecate in the open, promoting the behavioural change involved in purchasing, using, and maintaining a reinvented toilet will be a challenge.

The RTTC has inspired a number of innovative approaches, including sand filtration and smouldering, as well as electrochemical generation of hydrogen and hydrothermal carbonization of waste sludge. These are technological approaches that are currently not in use in the developed world. Once developed, however, these approaches can be just as useful in the developed world as they are in the developing world. Off-grid toilets can be useful in Canadian cottages, remote communities in the Canadian north, and cities or towns that are prone to flooding, to name just a few possibilities. This is an example where innovations motivated by the needs of the South may turn out to benefit the North.

Who Are the Innovators?

Progress in the development of appropriate technologies requires innovators, and while efforts directed at innovations in appropriate technologies for the Global South are disproportionately small compared to innovations for the Global North, there is a growing community of innovators, coming from different backgrounds and walks of life, who are focusing on designing for the "other 90 per cent."

Grassroots innovators driven by the challenges of their own work environment are the most inspiring. Dr Oluyombo Awojobi, a surgeon in rural Nigeria, has several inventions aimed at improving surgery in the rural setting in which he works. His inventions include an instrument for determining blood haematocrit using a manually powered centrifuge, based on bicycle gears and chains, that generates up to 3000G,[36] an operating table using a car jack,[37] and a foot-powered pedal suction pump. He is relentlessly focused on simplicity. In his words, *"the moment my proposed solution becomes more complex, I realize I have missed the road ... and I go back to basics."*[38] The emergence of websites such as AfriGadget.com, which highlights examples of African ingenuity, and Appropedia.org, an online Wiki of appropriate technologies, as well as new online communities for innovators to engage with one another such as Engineering for Change (E4C), bears witness to the plethora of grassroots innovation that is sparking interest around the globe.

Students, through classes or extracurricular organizations, have emerged as passionate innovators of simple appropriate technologies, and are making significant contributions through their efforts. Students from MIT's D-Lab, Stanford's D.School, Engineers Without Borders, Engineering World Health, and many others are making contributions using their design skills and engineering knowledge. For example, Robert Borden of North Carolina State University turned an idea about using augering to empty pit latrines into a BMGF funded project and his own Master's thesis.

Engineering World Health is a student organization that compiles a list of "Projects that Matter" and runs a design competition to mobilize student groups to address global health needs. Significant contributions (their "legacy projects") include surgical light bulbs, a spectrometer based on LEDs, and a temperature control system for baby incubators.

The Centre for Global Engineering at the University of Toronto offers courses aimed at the design of appropriate technologies, as well as an interdisciplinary course for addressing global challenges.

There is also significant capacity in innovation among academics and researchers from the Global South. K. Siddique-e Rabbani of the University of Dhaka in Bangladesh is working on research ranging from Focused Impedance Method (FIM) (a form of electrical impedance measurement) for diagnostic purposes to the development of low-cost, domestic-scale safe drinking water systems.

Global North researchers and well-connected/high-capacity researchers in the South (many of whom have spent time in international universities) have been motivated by funding sources such as the Bill and Melinda Gates Foundation and, more recently, Grand Challenges Canada. BMGF, GCC, the United States Agency for International Development (USAID), and the World Health Organization (WHO) have made a tremendous effort to mobilize research talent from around to world to develop innovative solutions to global development and global health issues. BMGF's Grand Challenges Exploration (GCE) program seeks innovations wherever they may arise. GCC seeks to motivate young researchers to work on global health issues through their Stars in Global Health program, as well as to promote North-South partnerships with a requirement in their topic-based programs that principal investigators must be from low- or middle-income countries (LMICs).

BMGF has funded global health researchers for more than a decade, while their recent RTTC has mobilized engineers and scientists from around the world, including many who had not been active in research on engineering solutions for the developing world. The RTTC was designed to entice engineering research talent in these schools to address an enormous need that had somehow been neglected among researchers. In bringing researchers from outside the field to address the sanitation challenge, it was hoped that out-of-the-box solutions would emerge.

The needs of the Global South combined with the support of donor organizations are spurring innovation from a wide range of individuals and groups globally. Grassroots projects inspired by local needs, student projects motivated by the opportunity to make a global impact, and academic projects for building research platforms to tackle complex engineering challenges are all leading to new and appropriate technologies for the Global South.

The Innovation Process – Making Innovation More Efficient and Scalable

Because of the enormous needs in the Global South, there are some who discount the need for technological innovations. For example, the focus of the Gates Foundation on technological solutions for global health and global development, while it has been a great motivation for innovators, has drawn criticism from others. In particular, the high-profile nature of the Reinvent the Toilet Challenge has focused critics' eyes on the various technological approaches that are being investigated. Some have argued that solutions such as pit latrines already exist and that the focus should be on implementing and scaling up such solutions. Others have criticized, even ridiculed, some of the technical approaches as being too complex. While it is true that, in these early days of RTTC, some of the technical approaches are too complex (the CGEN team's approach has elements of complexity that are being simplified), the criticism overlooks the fact that innovation processes are by their very nature not neat or efficient. Even when the goal of a simple and extremely affordable technical solution is clear, one does not progress directly to a simple solution, as evidenced by recent challenges faced by DataWind and their affordable tablet. Manufacturing capability in India is behind that of China, and the sheer numbers required to date make local manufacture in India a distant reality if the target tablet price is to be met. Manufacturing had to be moved to China in the fall of 2012 to meet the Indian government's order. Criticism of the project's overall premise, emerging in hindsight after the $100 One Laptop per Child initiative, is another hurdle that this company is currently addressing. It is common for innovations to go through many iterations, as approaches are tested and either rejected or refined, until a simple, workable solution is found. Expecting innovators to come up with a fully formed, simple, final product without iterations is analogous to asking a writer to compose a publishable novel in his first draft.

Even as we rebut criticism regarding the complexity of some of the technical approaches and argue for the intrinsic inefficiency and iterative nature of innovation processes, there is a source of inefficiency in innovation of appropriate technologies that is not intrinsic and that should be possible to overcome: that of the inefficiency of communication and knowledge sharing in this sphere.

Researchers who are part of the global network of knowledge creators have access to a tremendous amount of information – via journals, books, the Internet, personal and professional contacts, and so on. We know how to identify needs, or how to ask the next scientific question in a given field; we know what has been done and can take advantage of the work of other researchers. By contrast, the first challenge with innovations in appropriate technologies is to identify needs and to match innovators with those needs. Dr Oluyombo Awojobi is a rare individual who can come up with inventions to address the needs of his own rural surgery practice – and to speak about them globally. There are likely many global needs, small and large, that no one has written about and that have therefore not attracted the attention of innovators.

Even when solutions already exist, people who are not plugged into the global community are unlikely either to publicize their own innovations or to become aware of solutions that have been developed by others. How many rural doctors might be able to benefit from Dr Awojobi's bicycle-gear-driven haematocrit measuring device if they knew about it? How many hospitals around the world do not know about the training curricula that are being developed to train technicians to maintain equipment? Some conferences (e.g., the Appropriate Healthcare Technology Conference hosted by the Institution for Engineering Technology [IET] and the Institute of Electrical and Electronics Engineers' [IEEE] Global Humanitarian Technology Conference) and journals (e.g., the *International Journal for Service Learning in Engineering: Humanitarian Engineering and Social Entrepreneurship* [*IJSLE*] and the *Journal of Humanitarian Engineering* [*JHE*]) are emerging for communities of innovators to exchange ideas and share knowledge. Efforts to link communities are emerging as well: for example, the Engineering for Change online community and a notable initiative, Sustainable Sanitation Alliance (SuSanA), which recently merged with BMGF's Sanitation Network. SuSanA is now the go-to place for sanitation researchers, community workers, and businesses to network. However, such conferences, networks, and knowledge dissemination forums remain relatively small in number and scale compared to their counterparts in "mainstream" science and engineering fields.

Such networks, as well as high-quality conferences and journals, are essential to disseminate formal and informal knowledge efficiently, and to raise the standards for innovations, and, in turn, catalyse the acceleration and scale-up of innovations in appropriate technologies in various sectors. The need for improved knowledge dissemination mechanisms remains a key issue in the effort to scale up innovations for the Global South.

Conclusions

The needs and challenges in global health and global development are enormous. For engineers from the Global North, the challenges are (1) to identify significant needs that we may not be aware of, and (2) to understand the practical and cultural contexts within which the innovative products and processes will be used. The challenge is especially great when the design and development process is occurring far from the sites of intended use. Working with an interdisciplinary team can help engineers who are used to dealing primarily with technical issues to understand the needs of users in unfamiliar contexts, and to focus engineering designs in ways that will facilitate implementation and motivate user adoption. The challenge of designing for people who are not familiar with sanitation technologies but who can be motivated to use toilets if the toilets are convenient, culturally appropriate, and provide value such as energy, fertilizers, and clean water is different from the challenge of designing when only technical factors need to be considered. Integrated innovation that takes account of the technical, business, and social domains will increase the chances of developing more appropriate technologies.

THE IDEA IN BRIEF

A technology is appropriate if it is used for its intended purpose by the intended target users. Technologies often fail or are ineffective because they are not appropriate for the local context – that is they are incompatible with social, cultural, financial, or infrastructural realities.

IMPLICATIONS

1 Innovators must understand the needs and the context of the target users in order to develop appropriate technologies.
2 Technologies can be appropriate if they are compatible with cultural norms, motivate behaviour change by introducing a value proposition, or leverage cutting-edge technological advances if no solution has existed before.
3 Spending meaningful time with users and local partners to understand the local context is an essential part of the appropriate technology innovation process.

FOOD FOR THOUGHT

Insufficient knowledge sharing can significantly impede the development of appropriate technologies. Global North innovators need an in-depth understanding of the target context and users; and Global South innovators need support from global partnerships and collaborations to facilitate the innovation process. How can we best bridge this global divide?

REFERENCES

1 Hum, R.J., Jha, P., McGahan, A.M., & Cheng, Y.-L. (2012). "Global divergence in critical income for adult and childhood survival: Analyses of mortality using Michaelis-Menten." *eLife* 1 (December): e00051.

2 KickStart. (2013). Retrieved 5 January 2013 from www.kickstart.org.

3 Perry, L., & Malkin, R. (2011). "Effectiveness of medical equipment donations to improve health systems: How much medical equipment is broken in the developing world?" *Medical and Biological Engineering and Computing* 49: 719–22.

4 Malkin, R.A. (2007). "Design of health care technologies for the developing world." *Annual Review of Biomedical Engineering* 9 (5): 67–87; and Bustamante, K.D., Comaduran, D., Rodriguez, B.A., Aguilar, R., Nevarez, D., & Hernandez, L.C. (2012). "Medical equipment conditions for underserved rural hospitals in Chihuahua, Mexico." In *The 7th International Appropriate Healthcare Technologies Conference – World Health and Wellbeing for Developing Countries*. London, U.K.

5 Schumacher, E.F. (1973). *Small is beautiful: A study of economics as if people mattered*. London: Blond and Briggs.

6 Soman, D. (2013). "Behaviourally informed innovation." See chapter 2 in this book.

7 Compton, B., & Thatcher, A. (2012). "Increasing responsible donations of medical surplus." In *The 7th International Appropriate Healthcare Technologies Conference – World Health and Wellbeing for Developing Countries*, London, U.K.; and Jeandron, A., Page, M., Comte, B., & Blanc-Gonnet, C. (2012). "Improving practices in medical equipment support projects." In *The 7th International Appropriate Healthcare Technologies Conference – World Health and Wellbeing for Developing Countries*, London, U.K.

8 Howie, S.R., Hill, S.E., Peel, D., Sanneh, M., Njie, M., Hill, P.C., et al. (2008). "Beyond good intentions: Lessons on equipment donation from an African hospital." *Bulletin of the World Health Organization* 86: 52–6.

9 Peel, D., & Howie, S.R. (2009). "Oxygen concentrators for use in tropical countries: A Survey." *Journal of Clinical Engineering* (October–December): 205–9.

10 La Vincente, S.F., Peel, D., Carai, S., Weber, M.W., Enarson, P., Maganga, E., et al. (2011). "The functioning of oxygen concentrators in resource-limited settings: A situation assessment in two countries." *International Journal of Tuberculosis and Lung Disease* 15 (5): 693–9.

11 Bradley, B., Cheng, Y.-L., Peel, D., Mullally, S., & Howie, S.R. (2011). "Assessment of power availability and development of a low-cost battery-powered

medical oxygen delivery system: For use in low-resource health facilities in developing countries" In *IEEE Global Humanitarian Technology Conference*, Seattle, WA.

12 Bradley, B.D., Qu, S., Peel, D., Howie, S.R., & Cheng, Y.-L. (2012). "Storing oxygen or storing energy: A cost-effectiveness model for comparing appropriate medical oxygen supply systems in low-resource health facilities with intermittent power." In *The 7th International Appropriate Healthcare Technologies Conference – World Health and Wellbeing for Developing Countries*, London, U.K.

13 World Health Organization. (2011). "Medical device donations: Considerations for solicitation and provision." Geneva: WHO Press.

14 World Health Organization. (2011). "Health technology assessment of medical devices." Geneva: WHO Press.

15 Mullally, S., Bbuku, T., Musonda, G., & Measure, E. (2012). "Biomedical engineering technologist (BMET) curriculum and programme development in Zambia." In *The 7th International Appropriate Healthcare Technologies Conference – World Health and Wellbeing for Developing Countries*, London, U.K.

16 Malkin, R.A., & Perry, L. (2012). "Evaluation of the impact of a new biomedical equipment technician curriculum in Rwanda." In *The 7th International Appropriate Healthcare Technologies Conference – World Health and Wellbeing for Developing Countries*, London, U.K.

17 Zaman, M.H. (2012). "Biomedical engineering education in resource-limited settings: Creating an innovation eco-system." In *The 7th International Appropriate Healthcare Technologies Conference – World Health and Wellbeing for Developing Countries*, London, U.K.

18 Daglish, S.C., Hilditch, M., & Okunzi, J. (2012). "Development of a self-sustaining biomedical engineering training course in Uganda." In *The 7th International Appropriate Healthcare Technologies Conference – World Health and Wellbeing for Developing Countries*, London, U.K.

19 Gammie, A., Upadhayaya, M., Shrestha, S., & Zimmermann, M. (2012). "BMEAT Nepal – Assistant technician training for resource-poor settings." In *The 7th International Appropriate Healthcare Technologies Conference – World Health and Wellbeing for Developing Countries*, London, U.K.

20 Malkin, R.A., & Perry, L. (2012). "Evaluation of the impact of a new biomedical equipment technician curriculum in Rwanda."

21 Adjabu, N., Bradley, B., Gentles, B., Mullally, S., Ramirez, M., Renshaw, J., & Zienaa, J. (2012). "A Canadian-Ghanaian partnership for improving health technology management." In *The 7th International Appropriate*

Healthcare Technologies Conference – World Health and Wellbeing for Developing Countries, London, U.K.

22 Using a GBP to USD conversion rate of 1.6.

23 NHS Purchasing and Supply Agency. (2010). "Market review: Pulse oximeters in primary and prehospital care (CEP10066)." NHS Centre for Evidence-based Purchasing.

24 Colwell, R., Huq, A., Islam, M.S., Aziz, K.M.A., Yunus, M., Khan, N.H., et al. (2003). "Reduction of cholera in Bangladeshi villages by simple filtration." *Proceedings of the National Academy of Sciences (PNAS)* 100 (3): 1051–5.

25 Ibid.

26 Diosady, L.L., Alberti, J.O., Ramcharan, K., & Mannar, M.G. (2002). "Iodine stability in salt double-fortified with iron and iodine." *Food Nutrition Bulletin* 23 (2): 196–207; and Oshinowo, T., Diosady, L., Yusufali, R., & Laleye, L. (2004). "Stability of salt double-fortified with ferrous fumarate and potassium iodate or iodide under storage and distribution conditions in Kenya." *Food Nutrition Bulletin* 25 (3): 264–70.

27 Zimmermann, M.B., Zeder, C., Chaouki, N., Saad, A., Torresani, T., & Hurrell, R.F. (2003). "Dual fortification of salt with iodine and microencapsulated iron: A randomized, double-blind, controlled trial in Moroccan schoolchildren." *American Journal of Clinical Nutrition* 77 (2): 425–32.

28 Beinner, M.A., Velasquez-Meléndez, G., Pessoa, M.C., & Greiner, T. (2010). "Iron-fortified rice is as efficacious as supplemental iron drops in infants and young children." *Journal of Nutrition* 140 (1): 49–53; Li, Y.O., Lam, J., Diosady, L.L., & Jankowski, S. (2009). "Antioxidant system for the preservation of vitamin A in Ultra Rice." *Food Nutrition Bulletin* 30 (1): 82–9; and Hotz, C., Porcayo, M., Onofre, G., García-Guerra, A., Elliott, T., Jankowski, S., & Greiner, T. (2008). "Efficacy of iron-fortified Ultra Rice in improving the iron status of women in Mexico." *Food Nutrition Bulletin* 29 (2): 140–9.

29 Soman (2013), "Behaviourally informed innovation."

30 Ibid.

31 Schumacher (1973), *Small is beautiful.*

32 Polak, P. (2008). *Out of poverty: What works when traditional approaches fail.* San Francisco: Berrett-Koehler.

33 Soman (2013), "Behaviourally informed innovation."

34 Ibid.

35 Fu, E., Lutz, B., Kauffman, P., & Yager, P. (2010). "Controlled reagent transport in disposable 2D paper networks." *Lab on a Chip* 10: 918–20; and Yager, P., Gonzalo, J.D., & Gerdes, J. (2008). "Point-of-care diagnostics for global health." *Annual Review of Biomedical Engineering* 10: 107–44.

36 Awojobi, O.A. (2012). "The manual haematocrit centrifuge." *Tropical Doctor* 32: 168; and Awojobi, O.A. (2012). "Manual haematocrit centrifuge." In *The 7th International Appropriate Healthcare Technologies Conference – World Health and Wellbeing for Developing Countries*, London, U.K.

37 Awojobi, O.A. (1994). "Appropriate technology for operating tables." *Africa Health* 16: 17–19.

38 World Health Organization. (2010). "Rising to the challenge of rural surgery: An interview with Les Olson." *Bulletin of the World Health Organization* 88: 331–2.

4

Globalization of Biopharmaceutical Innovation: Implications for Poor-Market Diseases

RAHIM REZAIE

Introduction

Gross inequity in health is one of the greatest challenges facing humanity. While the average person born today in Canada, the United States, western Europe, Japan, and many other parts of the developed world can expect to live well into his or her eighties, in countries such as Zimbabwe, Mozambique, and Liberia life expectancy is about forty to fifty years, and in some cases falling. This disparity has many causes and consequences, but the overarching common element that distinguishes the latter group of countries from the former is economic prosperity, or lack thereof. We know that there is an intimate connection between health and wealth at both the individual and national levels, and that this relationship is self-reinforcing. Wealth can enhance health, and health is a prerequisite for wealth, broadly speaking. Where societies have made inroads against both somewhat simultaneously, the resulting dynamic has often created a virtuous cycle by making the healthy wealthier, and vice versa. Inequities in health arise from many factors that work together in complex ways. One important dimension, which I focus on in this chapter, is access to health technologies, particularly medicines, vaccines, and diagnostics, the development of which can be highly costly and time consuming.

There is no question that access or lack of access to health technologies and services is a major contributor to health inequity throughout the globe. In this respect the challenge, broadly speaking, is twofold: (1) how can we ensure that safe, efficacious, and appropriate solutions for the prevention or treatment of various human ailments – particularly those affecting the global poor – are developed in the first place; and (2) how can we ensure that, once developed, they reach all those who need them, regardless of geography or socio-economic status? For our purposes here we can think of the first as a largely scientific/technological challenge (or, as conceptualized by Cheng and Bradley in the preceding chapter, as aiming at appropriateness through engineering and design), and the second as largely a delivery problem (related to the presence of a support ecosystem, also discussed in the preceding chapter) – although in reality the two are highly interconnected.

This chapter takes off from the preceding one by discussing how engagement in the health innovation process itself by actors and institutions in resource-poor nations can lead to more appropriate and accessible technologies for use in such settings. Specifically, it is concerned with the challenges related to the development and provision of safe and efficacious vaccines, drugs, and diagnostics to meet the health needs of the global poor. The basic argument is that, in the context of knowledge-based and highly resource-intensive sectors such as biotechnology and pharmaceuticals (henceforth collectively referred to as the biopharmaceutical sector), our traditional notion of innovation as a place-based phenomenon is increasingly challenged by the globalization and disaggregation of innovation value chains, and that this has profound implications for economic development and global health. The growing participation of actors based in emerging markets within this global value chain is laying the groundwork for more appropriate health technologies by helping to minimize both innovation costs and mismatches between technologies and their target settings.

I briefly digress to clarify a couple of key concepts. The notion of a *value chain* is commonly used in the literature to encapsulate the collection of activities that add value in the process of converting some type of input(s) to output(s). As initially popularized by the renowned management scholar Michael Porter of Harvard University, these can be envisaged as activities either within a given firm or, more broadly, within a particular industrial sector. In terms of drug development, for example, the innovation value chain encompasses the totality of all activities, from the discovery of a promising drug candidate, to its testing, and the eventual marketing of the end product to patients. Historically, firm- and country-centric innovation has been the predominant mode in the biopharmaceutical industry, where a relatively small number of firms and countries have dominated the innovation landscape. A specific firm would either discover a promising drug candidate or license it from another firm, university, or research institute and then conduct most, if not all, of the downstream activities necessary to test, manufacture, and market the given vaccine or medicine. Where complex health technologies have resulted from collaboration among firms, they have almost exclusively involved firms in only a few industrialized nations. However, we are now witnessing the growing participation in the biopharmaceutical innovation value chain of researchers and companies based in key emerging markets – most prominently China and India – as well as in newly industrialized nations such as Taiwan, Singapore, South Korea, and Brazil. What this means is that the actual work involved in developing a specific heart medication, for example, might involve numerous firms and research institutions in several countries. In other words, value-adding innovative activities are increasingly disaggregated across firms or other entities in different countries. This phenomenon, which I refer to as the *disaggregation of the innovation value chain*, has profound implications for health technology innovation and the social and economic prosperity that can flow from it. While disruptive in some respects to Western innovation and business models, it is creating new opportunities for countries and companies in resource-constrained settings to participate in the innovation value chain.

Until very recently, almost all leading-edge knowledge and innovative capabilities have been sourced in the industrialized world; however, such capabilities are now appearing in leading emerging markets, including China, India, and Brazil.[1] Discussions in this chapter are informed by an analysis of the growth of biopharmaceutical innovation in the countries just mentioned. Despite being classified as middle-income countries in aggregate economic terms, these three nations collectively house a substantial portion of the global population that is considered to be ultra poor. As such, the diffusion of innovative activity to these and other proximal settings of poverty is likely to have considerable implications for the way in which local and global health needs are addressed.

Looked at from the perspective of innovations aimed at economic development broadly and the development of affordable and appropriate technologies specifically, the trend towards value chain disaggregation and globalization is creating new opportunities for both incumbent firms and nations. In essence, it allows for a strategy of "divide and conquer," with the following potential benefits: (a) a vastly expanded pool of innovators, ideas, and resources, particularly in and from poverty settings; (b) a more equitable distribution of innovation costs and benefits; (c) efficiency gains that can arise from specialization, economies of scale, and lower labour costs; (d) the development and adaptation of technologies to make them more appropriate for use in poverty settings: and (e) the opening of new paths to economic development for emerging markets and other developing nations vis-à-vis global value chains.

The chapter is organized as follows. First, I contextualize the discussion in light of the potential impact that health technology innovation can have in addressing needs of the global poor. Second, I present an overview of the prevalent drug development model, which I call the "Western innovation model," and the challenges that this approach faces with respect to research and development (R&D) productivity. Third, I take stock of relevant changes that are occurring in key emerging markets, particularly China, India, and Brazil, from the perspective of their attempts to enhance their own scientific and technological capabilities in general and to become more innovative in health technologies in particular. Fourth, I discuss how capabilities in the emerging markets mentioned (which for the sake of contrast I am calling the "East") are being integrated into the *Western* innovation model, resulting in a *disaggregated* and globalized innovation value chain. Lastly, I ponder the potential of this disaggregation and globalization of innovation activities in health technology for addressing health-care needs of the global poor.

Background: Health Technology Innovation and the Poor

The adverse distributive consequences of technological innovations in health arise to a significant extent from the fact that high-tech innovation has traditionally been the purview of developed nations, while developing countries served mainly as technology users, and as only secondary markets at that. Chapter 3 in this book identifies many concrete examples of how the disconnect between the supply and demand sectors has led to the development and provision of technologies that are often inappropriate for use in poverty settings. This mismatch has been particularly apparent in the biopharmaceutical sector, where firms in a few industrialized nations have dominated the innovation landscape for decades. The health and economic benefits of innovation have also been disproportionately skewed towards high-income countries, with the resultant innovations often inaccessible to hundreds of millions of people in developing countries. If this technological dependence were to continue, it has been argued, its distributive consequences would serve to exacerbate the existing inequalities between the developed and the developing nations, particularly in the context of the knowledge-based economy.[2]

As far as health technologies are concerned, a group of seventeen so-called neglected tropical diseases (NTDs) most clearly epitomize the challenge of unequal access to health technologies. The World Health Organization (WHO) estimates that these diseases alone affect more than one billion people annually. These are diseases that most of us living in the industrialized West have likely never heard of. They include Chagas disease, leishmaniasis, dengue fever, schistosomiasis, and others. They can cause anything from blindness to heart disease, and can often be fatal if untreated. Not included among NTDs are other major poverty diseases such as tuberculosis, malaria, HIV/AIDS, and various diarrheal and other transmissible diseases that affect hundreds of millions more in the developing world – including millions of children. Yet, the WHO also observes, only 16 of 1,393 new drugs marketed between 1975 and 1999 were for tropical diseases – a mere 1 per cent. Diagnostic and preventive solutions also often remain highly inadequate in settings of poverty. In the case of many NTDs, we have not invested sufficiently even in basic research, which means that the bill has been adding up all along. One consequence of this oversight is that current efforts to address NTDs must, in many cases, start from scratch – with understanding the biology of the disease, identifying disease targets and promising interventions, and demonstrating their safety and efficacy. Only then can efforts to ensure quality and achieve scaled manufacturing and marketing begin. The result is delays and the dilution of the often limited resources that go to solving these challenges.

What is more, in many ways neglected diseases are just the tip of the iceberg when it comes to our poor track record on innovating to meet the needs of the poor. Health technology innovation in the West has given us fairly safe and effective solutions for diabetes, cardiovascular disease, numerous infectious diseases, and many other ailments. No one calls these *neglected* diseases today. But if you travelled in sub-Saharan Africa, rural India, and many other regions in the developing world, you would be hard pressed to find many of the solutions that we in the West often take for granted widely available. For millions of the global poor there is not a great difference between diabetes and dengue, as far as their likelihood of getting appropriate treatments is concerned. Indeed there is evidence that developing countries sometimes pay more for medicines than developed ones. For example, a study comparing retail prices in Brazil and Sweden found that, for a basket of 132 essential medicines, Brazilians pay, on average, about twice as much as Swedes, an inequity that is magnified when we consider that per-capita income in Sweden is ten times that in Brazil.[3] This is notwithstanding the fact that Brazil has a vibrant domestic generic drug industry, an asset that is lacking in most resource-poor nations. Given the considerable and rising burden of chronic, non-communicable diseases in the developing world, the need for innovations – both technological and of other types – that make solutions more accessible is critical.[4] In 2011, 90 million people in China and 61.3 million in India had diabetes, resulting in approximately 1.3 and 1 million deaths in these countries, respectively.[5] Global prevalence is of course much higher and increasing due to rising affluence, as more people in the developing world join the middle class and in doing so consume more calories and lead more sedentary lives. The discussion that follows outlines how innovative solutions to some of these challenges are being developed, and, encouragingly, in settings where the need is greatest, such as China and India.

Why Has Health Innovation for the Poor Largely Eluded Us?

It is generally believed that developing solutions for diseases that predominantly affect economically impoverished populations has not appeared sufficiently profitable to attract interest from the private sector. This is a credible but incomplete explanation for why we do not have effective vaccines for malaria or drugs for dengue fever. Those who see the lack of private incentives as the primary reason – and many do – accept the notion that the global pharmaceutical industry has been both too profit-driven and too ignorant of the diseases of the poor to want to innovate in this area. They also argue that an industry that has produced highly effective solutions not only for infectious diseases that are prevalent in the Western world but also for heart disease and various cosmetic needs, but has chosen not to work on dengue fever, bears most of the responsibility for the omission. The solution then seems clear. The pharmaceutical industry – by which most generally mean large innovating biopharmaceutical multinational corporations (MNCs) – should start investing in poverty diseases. This suggestion seems intuitive until one considers the fact that our prevalent, and largely Western, drug development model gives us new drugs at an average up-front cost of approximately $600 million (U.S.), which is equivalent to approximately $1.2 billion (U.S.) when opportunity costs are factored in.[6] Suggestions that pooling poor-market needs through the expansion of intellectual property rights in settings of poverty (vis-à-vis adoption of the World Health Organization's TRIPS agreement) will stimulate new private investment in research into neglected diseases by multinational firms do not appear to be realistic.[7] Indeed, it has been suggested that enforcement of intellectual property rights in China and India may actually limit access to basic medicines for developing countries in general, at least over the short term.[8]

To be sure, some key pharmaceutical MNCs have responded to criticism by paying more attention to diseases that are prevalent in poor markets. As the Access to Medicine Foundation's *Access to Medicines Index Report 2012*[9] suggests, improvements are being made with respect to how innovating biopharmaceutical MNCs respond to issues of access for poor populations. However, given the scale of the challenge, more is needed. In short, we must expand our horizon beyond these firms if we are to find affordable, accessible, and sustainable solutions to pressing global health challenges. We cannot rely solely on costly innovations originating in the Global North to meet the needs of highly price-sensitive users in the Global South.

In essence, the challenge is to find new ways of ensuring that the person earning a few dollars per day has access to a drug or vaccine that cost hundreds of millions of dollars to develop, a challenge that cannot be divorced from broader industry evolution. This is a perplexing challenge to be sure, and the solution is especially difficult to imagine if we see things continuing as they have done in the past, with a relatively small number of firms in a handful of industrialized countries innovating for everyone else. To be fair, many firms and scientists in other countries have contributed to this system, but the top ten or twenty biopharmaceutical MNCs have for decades served as aggregators of knowledge and innovation in the field, and as key gatekeepers of consumer access. In the process, they have exerted considerable control and influence over how and where innovative activity takes place, and over who benefits and at what cost. Given their continued dominance of the global industry, any significant change in the broader industry structure at the global level will hinge on their choices and actions. As I argue below, such changes are happening, if more by necessity than by choice.

How to Innovate with the Poor End User in Mind?

At the outset, we must recognize that innovating for the poor does not necessarily mean innovating on the cheap. Developing safe and effective vaccines, medicines, and diagnostics is often highly costly, technologically challenging, and time consuming. Making vaccines that are heat-stable, so as not to require continuous refrigeration, or drugs that can withstand sustained ·and high levels of heat and humidity adds costs to innovations for the poor. Other examples, including point-of-care diagnostics, lab-on-chip technologies, and efforts to reinvent the toilet, have been discussed in the preceding chapter. Making these and other health technologies more appropriate to developing world contexts can often require additional resources beyond what it would normally cost to develop a product for use in the industrialized world where delivery infrastructure is well established. Add to these complexities the growing burden of non-communicable diseases and it quickly becomes apparent that the health-care challenges faced by the billions of people who earn only a few dollars a day are not going to be solved by temporary fixes, philanthropic funds, or development assistance alone. A fundamentally new approach is required that utilizes resources more strategically, is explicitly focused on the needs of the poor, and is in line with how the industry is evolving and with opportunities arising from the globalization of science, technology, and commerce. In the context of resource-intensive health technologies, to advance the agenda of innovating for the poor is to imagine a radically different industry configuration – with a cost structure, profit expectation, and geographic distribution of innovation activity quite unlike the one we have become accustomed to.

The Western Biopharmaceutical Innovation Model

The modern pharmaceutical industry began in the first half of the twentieth century in Germany and Switzerland, where the medicinal effects of some dyestuffs became apparent to the local synthetic dye industries. Mass production of the antibiotic penicillin during the Second World War, commissioned for the armed forces by the U.S. government, was a major turning point for the industry. The decades that followed saw a stream of new medicines being marketed by major U.S.-based companies such as Merck, Eli Lilly, Bristol-Myers, and Pfizer, all of which have remained dominant players in the global pharmaceutical industry. In the 1970s, the discovery of recombinant DNA technology led to the emergence of a new crop of biotechnology firms. Again dominated by a relatively few large firms – such as Genentech (in San Francisco, but now part of Roche based in Basel, Switzerland) and Amgen (in Thousand Oaks, California) – but also populated by many small companies, this sector is increasingly integrated with the more traditional pharmaceutical companies. Together these constitute what I collectively call the biopharmaceutical industry.

The sustained dominance of a relatively small number of global biopharmaceutical firms means that a handful of countries, including the United States, the United Kingdom, Switzerland, Germany, and France, have been dominant forces in biopharmaceutical innovation – albeit with considerable scientific and technological input from several other countries. In general, differential institutional contexts are credited for this concentration of health technology innovation in a relatively few countries.[10] Institutional dimensions related to knowledge creation, intellectual property ownership and management, and the regulation of product safety and efficacy have been particularly crucial in this respect.

Historically, the prevalent drug development model has relied on three key pillars, described in more detail below. However, these pillars are now being compromised, with the net effect of changing the global industry structure as a whole, including rebalancing health technology innovation in terms of where it happens, who participates in the innovation value chain and how, and, ultimately, who benefits.

The first pillar supporting the Western innovation model has been a captive and affluent Western consumer market that, for decades, has been willing to pay high prices for health technologies. The ability to reap large margins has in turn enhanced the ability of firms to invest considerable sums in research and development (R&D). For example, Novartis and Pfizer spend approximately $8 to $10 billion (U.S.) in R&D each year. However, faced with rising and unsustainable health costs, many industrialized countries are beginning to look for savings. In 2010, the United States dedicated 17.6 per cent of its aggregated GDP to health expenditures, amounting to an annual per-capita expenditure of $8,233 (www.oecd.org). Other major OECD countries (such as Germany, France, the United Kingdom, and Canada) spend somewhat less – about 10 to 12 per cent of GDP – but are also facing cost increases that are well above normal inflation. These factors are putting pressure on drug prices, and may as a result affect the ability of pharmaceutical companies to fund new innovations. In addition, growth rates in the pharmaceutical market are stagnating in most industrialized countries, leaving emerging markets as the settings that offer substantial growth prospects over the coming years.[11]

The second pillar supporting the Western innovation model was the high number of new innovations produced by the pharmaceutical sector in the decades following the Second World War, a level of innovation that is becoming increasingly hard to sustain. Notwithstanding early successes in bringing many products to market, over the past ten to fifteen years the sector has faced considerable productivity deficits characterized by diminishing returns on R&D expenditures. The U.S. biopharmaceutical sector alone spent about $117 billion on R&D in 2010 and 2011(www.phrma.org), during which only fifty-six new drugs were approved by the Food and Drug Administration, a number that includes innovations by all companies globally, not just in the United States (www.fda.gov). As was mentioned earlier, the average cost per drug now exceeds $1 billion (U.S.). Therefore, the Western drug development model, which has long been unaffordable for millions in the developing countries, is now becoming increasingly unaffordable in rich countries also. As a result, the industry as a whole is looking for new approaches to address its productivity deficit, in part by undertaking innovative activities in new places, most prominently in the Asia-Pacific region.

The third key pillar supporting the Western innovation model has been the ability of firms to raise sufficient private capital to finance costly R&D activities. This aspect has been particularly important in nurturing the modern biotechnology industry that increasingly feeds new technologies into the pipelines of large biopharmaceutical MNCs. The financing model has relied substantially on robust regimes for the protection of intellectual property in the United States and other industrialized economies. Rising innovation costs, pressure on pharmaceutical prices, the global financial-sector crisis, and the fact that patent terms are running out for many blockbuster drugs are making it increasingly challenging for Western innovators to fund innovative projects, precisely at a time when development costs are at their peak and rising.

There have been a number of attempts at addressing the pharmaceutical industry's productivity deficit in recent decades. The first major attempt by larger biopharmaceutical MNCs involved mergers and acquisitions. The basic rationale was that the larger the firm the more it could optimize its assets and distribute costs over many products and product categories. In theory, this made some sense. In practice, we have seen continued R&D productivity declines over the past two decades in the face of many mergers and acquisitions that have made some MNCs among the largest companies in the world. At present, the industry as a whole and large biopharmaceutical MNCs in particular are experimenting with a range of options, among them the outsourcing of R&D and manufacturing activities, the in- and out-licensing of technologies, and the co-development and joint marketing of products with other firms and agencies all over the world. For example, a U.K. study found that approximately a quarter of all R&D expenditures (amounting to about $1.6 billion [U.S.] in 2005) occurred outside the country, a trend that is influenced by local firms' interest in reducing development times and costs and in accessing related expertise.[12] We also know that the complexity and multidisciplinary nature of biopharmaceutical innovation makes these firms significantly more dependent on external sources of knowledge, hence enhancing the likelihood of external collaborations.[13] Large global firms are also increasingly operating their own R&D facilities in emerging markets, especially China and India. For instance, Novartis announced in 2009 that it plans to invest $1.25 billion (U.S.) in two R&D facilities in China, and Pfizer, which had about 340 employees at its Shanghai-based R&D centre in the same year, announced in 2011 that it will move its antibacterial research from the United States and the United Kingdom to China. The internationalization of corporate R&D activities is not new. What is new, and in some ways different, is the location of R&D activities and the reasons that underlie the diffusion of innovation activity. Historically, it has been argued that companies that are highly internationalized tend to conduct activities that bolster their competitive position at home.[14] But with growth prospects in the biopharmaceutical sector now largely confined to emerging markets, these efforts are increasingly motivated by different forces, including considerations of market access.

At its core, the Western biopharmaceutical model has relied heavily on an integrated company model, where large firms internalized most of the necessary research, preclinical, clinical, and marketing capabilities to bring new drugs to market. This model has proved to be very expensive and increasingly unsustainable, particularly from the perspective of supporting innovations for the poor.

Rising Innovative Capability in the "East"

As mentioned previously, in recent decades innovation in the biopharmaceutical sector has largely been the purview of Western companies and countries. However, we are now seeing a diffusion of innovative activities to a growing number of emerging markets. These efforts are most significant in leading emerging markets such as China, India, and Brazil. Over the past six years, I and various colleagues have studied dozens of indigenous companies in the stated countries, and the observations in this chapter draw much from insights gained through that process. In a series of studies, led by Dr Peter Singer of the University of Toronto, we show that domestic companies in the stated markets are making substantial contributions to addressing local and global health needs, both through innovation and by offering existing products to local populations at more affordable prices.[15] These studies have helped to expose the considerable national effort in many parts of the world to enhance innovation capacity in health technology. We also elaborate on the extent and nature of health technology innovations in the relevant countries, and argue that, as a group, firms in emerging markets constitute an important but hitherto largely untapped resource for addressing global health challenges.[16] We suggest that local governments, international aid agencies, and the global health community at large should utilize the largely untapped innovation potential of the entrepreneurial sectors in emerging markets in order to advance such innovations.

The relatively recent foray into innovation activity by emerging market countries is a radical departure from past practice, and therefore will take some time to develop fully. Historically, Indian, Chinese, and Brazilian firms began with the low-cost manufacturing of vaccines, drugs, and diagnostics for local (and in some cases global) populations. In almost all cases, they copied innovations made elsewhere and, through reverse engineering and process innovations, made many health technologies more accessible for millions in the developing world. The overall approach of domestic firms in India – and to a lesser extent China and Brazil – over the past decade has been an ambitious attempt at building capabilities to serve not only the domestic but also the global pharmaceutical market. For instance, large Indian firms such as Ranbaxy (based in Gurgao, now part of Japan's Daiichi Sankyo), Wockhardt (Mumbai), and Dr Reddy's Laboratories (Hyderabad) already sell dozens of medicinal products in the United States, Europe, and other parts of the industrialized and developing world. Today India has the largest number of FDA-compliant manufacturing laboratories for medicines outside the United States itself, a fact that facilitates medicinal exports to the United States and elsewhere.

Science and Technology Progress in Emerging Markets

Four main factors have contributed to science and technology development in emerging markets in general and to biopharmaceutical innovation in particular. First and foremost, continued economic growth and relative macroeconomic stability over the past few decades have enhanced the ability of governments and entrepreneurs in China, India, and Brazil to increase investments in R&D and other innovation-enhancing activities. The UNESCO Science Report (2010) shows that between the years 2000 and 2008, China's R&D expenditures grew an average of 23 per cent to reach $66.5 billion (U.S.), or 1.5 per cent of GDP in 2008. Although as a portion of GDP India's and Brazil's R&D expenditures remained fairly constant (at 1 per cent and 0.8 per cent, respectively), GDP growth has nonetheless translated into a near doubling of India's spending between 2002 and 2007, to $24 billion (U.S.), while Brazil's expenditures stood at $20.3 billion at the end of this period.

Second, sustained and growing investment in science and technology has enhanced the capacity for knowledge generation in these countries. Judging by expenditures in research and development, scientific publication trends, and domestic patenting, leading emerging markets are making significant strides, and in some cases, particularly China, are fast catching up to the leading industrialized nations. As shown in figure 4.1 and table 4.1, key developing economies overall, and China, India, and Brazil in particular, have increased their scientific publication output significantly relative to leading industrialized nations such as the United States, Japan, and Germany. For instance, scientific publications by researchers in developing countries more than doubled between 2002 and 2008 but expanded by only 20 per cent in developed markets. In China, the increase in the scale and speed of scientific publication is particularly striking.

Third, all three countries, China, India, and Brazil, have witnessed a dramatic shift in the attitude of the state towards industry over the past two decades. China has seen an evolution from outright prohibition of private enterprise about two decades ago to state subsidization of R&D activities within many private companies. Indian and Brazilian government responses have been less dramatic in scale but in general have become more supportive as well, and in many respects mimic those of China and other industrialized nations. These efforts are motivated not only by the demand for health technologies but also by the recognition that innovation is key to sustained economic growth.

Figure 4.1. Scientific Publication in Select Developed and Developing Economies (1998–2012)

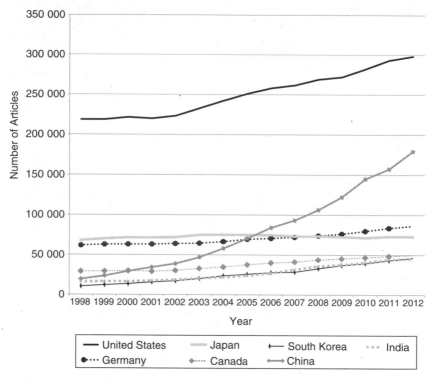

Data Source: Science Citation Index Expanded (SCI-EXPANDED), Web of Knowledge

Lastly, globalization forces combined with these three countries' intrinsic desire to become innovative have induced institutional changes in key areas, including the protection of intellectual property (IP), that have created a more favourable environment for innovation. Adoption of the World Trade Organization's TRIPS (Trade-related Aspects of Intellectual Property Rights) agreement has changed the equation drastically for domestic sectors in the emerging economies. There is a broad recognition among emerging market entrepreneurs that the long-term growth and competitiveness of health enterprises in these settings now depend, to a significant extent, on their ability to generate and extract value from intellectual property (IP). Figure 4.2 shows changes in patenting across different countries classified by income, as well as in

Table 4.1 Change in Scientific Publication Patterns across Various Countries and Regions from 2002 to 2008

Region / Country Grouping	Total Publications (No. of Papers)		Change (%)	Share of World Publications (%)		Biomedical Research Publications (No. of Papers)	
	2002	2008	2002–2008	2002	2008	2002	2008
World	733,305	986,099	34.5	100	100	99,805	123,316
Developed Countries	617,879	742,256	20.1	84.3	75.3	89,927	100,424
Developing Countries	153,367	315,742	105.9	20.9	32	14,493	32,091
Least Developed Countries	2,069	3,766	82	0.3	0.4	226	471
North America	250,993	306,676	22.2	34.2	31.1	44,700	49,590
Europe	333,317	419,454	25.8	45.5	42.5	43,037	50,464
Africa	11,776	19,650	66.9	1.6	2	1,122	2,397
Asia	177,743	303,147	70.6	24.2	30.7	19,022	31,895
Japan	73,429	74,618	1.6	10	7.6	9,723	9,771
China	38,206	104,968	174.7	5.2	10.6	2,682	9,098
India	18,911	36,261	91.7	2.6	3.7	1,901	3,821
Newly Industrialized Economies in Asia	33,765	62,855	86.2	4.6	6.4	3,240	6,795
Brazil	12,573	26,482	110.6	1.7	2.7	1,583	3,467
Canada	30,310	43,539	43.6	4.1	4.4	4,779	6,018
France	47,219	57,133	21	6.4	5.8	6,563	7,169
Germany	65,500	76,368	16.6	8.9	7.7	8,742	10,006
United Kingdom	61,073	71,302	16.7	8.3	7.2	9,586	10,789

Source: Data Reconfigured from UNESCO Science Report 2010.

Figure 4.2. Patent Applications by Country Grouping Based on Economic Status. The United States and China presented separately also for comparison (Direct and PCT national phase entries count by applicants origin) (2000–2011)

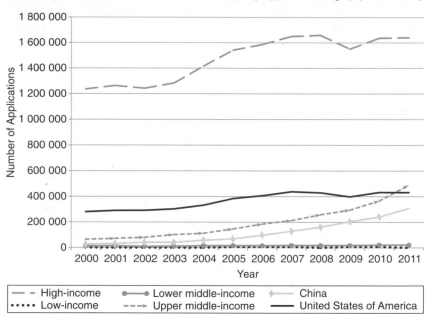

Data source: http://ipstatsdb.wipo.org/ipstats

China and the United States individually. It shows that, as a group, high-income countries continue to maintain a substantial lead in terms of patent applications, followed by upper-middle-income nations. However, as the figure also shows, China is by far the main driver of patenting growth in the upper-middle-income category, having overtaken the United States in numbers of applications submitted to its patent office in 2011. One can argue about the quality of Chinese patents relative to those in other industrialized nations, but the trend as a whole is unambiguous and reflects the country's strengthening science and technology capacity and emphasis on patenting.

An Emerging "East-West" Model: Towards Disaggregated Innovation

There are clear indications that biopharmaceutical innovation activity is disaggregating. This disaggregation is evidenced not only by the emerging capacity for innovation in new settings but also by the way in which individual drugs, vaccines, or other complex technologies are actually being developed. Qualitative evidence points to the involvement of more firms and research institutions in the development of individual products than ever before. These actors and institutions are also increasingly located in a wider range of countries than before. China and India – and other key Asian economies such as Taiwan, Singapore, and South Korea – are among the key players in this respect and are entering the biopharmaceutical innovation landscape at a time when the nature of the game is changing rapidly. The new and emerging paradigm can be characterized as a globally fragmented drug development value chain with greater participation by emerging markets than ever before.

A disaggregated value chain provides many entry and exit points, allowing large and small firms to participate by specializing in distinct domains without having to incur the significant costs involved in the integrated innovation model that aims to achieve efficiencies through economies of scale and scope. A disaggregated value chain takes advantage of economies of scale through specialization of pure-play firms that add incremental value to the eventual innovation. An analogy may be found in the Blackberry or iPhone smartphones. These devices, although marketed by specific firms, are by-products of input from many firms in several countries. They are compilations of hundreds of individual components and technologies that in fact originate from dozens of firms and other entities throughout the globe. This general pattern towards disaggregation of innovation activities is increasingly taking hold in the biopharmaceutical sector as well, although the speed of progress in this direction is slower and hence less evident to casual observers. Nonetheless, this shift has far-reaching consequences for both incumbent innovators and newcomers to the game.

Indeed, the drive towards biopharmaceutical innovation by domestic firms, particularly in China and India, is facilitated to a considerable degree by their integration into the global biopharmaceutical innovation value chain. As such, enhanced scientific and technological capacity in emerging markets is helping to reshape how innovation takes place within the resource-intensive global biopharmaceutical industry as a whole. Not only are most large firms establishing a significant presence in key emerging markets, they are collaborating with and outsourcing a growing portion of their R&D activities to domestic firms in these settings. Advinus Therapeutics (Bangalore) and Wuxi PharmaTech (Shanghai) lead fast-growing R&D services companies in China and India that cater largely to biopharmaceutical MNCs. Indian companies such as Biocon (Bangalore), Suven Life Sciences (Hyderabad), Serum Institute of India (Pune), Piramal Life Sciences (Mumbai); China-based firms such as Shanghai Genomics and Hutchison Medipharma (Shanghai); and Brazil-based FK Biotech (Porto Alegre) and Aché Laboratories (São Paulo) are among a growing crop of firms that engage in both collaborative and independent innovation projects with foreign counterparts and in some cases provide R&D services to them as well.

Moreover, the rising innovation capability in emerging markets is not just a domestic story. Increasing innovation capacity in Asia and elsewhere serves several purposes for biopharmaceutical MNCs. It not only offers the prospect of lower innovation costs, it also provides the MNCs with a bargaining tool in dealing with Western economies. As Jon Symonds, Global Finance Director for Novartis, which spends about $10 billion (U.S.) on R&D each year, recently warned the British government, *"one of the characteristics of the UK is a very low up-take on innovation ... sitting in another part of the business allocating my resources, if we don't see the up-take in the UK resources will be allocated elsewhere."*[17] This warning followed Pfizer's decision in 2011 to close its last R&D facility in Britain, eliminating 2,400 jobs in the process, a step that the company attributed to its global program of change and overall reduction in R&D expenditure.[18] GlaxoSmithKline (GSK) recently announced job cuts in Australia, where Geoff McDonald, GSK's general manager said, *"Funding for medicines is currently very challenging in Australia."*[19] Similar scenarios are unfolding elsewhere also, as the global competition for skilled, high-paying jobs intensifies among nations, regions, and individual cities.

Disaggregated Innovation: Potential for Innovation for the Poor

Lingering uncertainties notwithstanding, the emerging innovation model is promising in at least three respects. First, this model is more enabling to a new, large, and expanding cohort of innovators in emerging markets and other developing countries. To the extent that it is inclusive of actors in low-resource settings and responsive to the specific needs of these markets, it is also a more *embedded* approach to innovation (a topic that is discussed more fully in the following chapter). This inclusive innovation approach has the effect of expanding the global pool of innovators and enabling new approaches to innovation, developments that, at least theoretically, should result in greater innovation outcomes. Second, the model brings together complementary resources from different parts of the world in the interest of more cost-effective innovation; for instance, technology from the West and low-cost manufacturing in the East. Collaborative partnerships provide greater opportunities for companies and researchers in the industrialized world to gain access to patients, cost-effective R&D, and marketing capabilities in emerging markets. In turn, domestic companies, in China and India for instance, can gain access to complementary technologies and know-how to help develop their own innovative products sooner and tap new sources of financing.

Third, greater engagement of innovators at the coalface of global health challenges should make the overall innovation system more cognizant of the needs of the poor and facilitate an increase in innovations to meet those needs. The shift to global innovation has the potential to create considerable opportunities – particularly for latecomer nations and businesses. It has the potential to accelerate drug development, reduce innovation costs, enhance therapeutic choice, and, ultimately, make end products more affordable to populations in the developing world.

Abdallah Daar and Peter Singer, in their recent book *The Grandest Challenge: Taking Life-Saving Science from Lab to Village,* argue that innovating for the poor involves taking the lab closer to the village.[20] Recent analysis suggests that indigenous firms in the emerging markets of China, India, and Brazil show an interest in addressing locally relevant health challenges. Anecdotal evidence also suggests that, even when focused on global diseases, the approximately 100 emerging market firms that we have studied show an interest, as a group, in diseases that are relevant to local conditions. Indian companies, for instance, have a major focus on diabetes, and Chinese firms on hepatitis, diseases that are particularly prevalent in their respective societies. And this local focus is not just the result of enhanced empathy or awareness of needs. The interest in finding solutions to local challenges is to a large extent accounted for by the fact that the value proposition, profit expectation, and cost structures for domestic companies in these settings are qualitatively different than they are for multinational corporations and other Western-based firms. As Dr Fernando Kreutz, president of Brazil-based FK Biotech, told us, "*What you call a neglected disease, I call a business opportunity.*" Ms Kiran Mazumdar-Shah, the CEO of India-based Biocon, shares this interest in the needs of local patients: "*There is no point to find ... costly wonder drug[s] ... that [are] not going to find their way to patients who need them.*" To Mazumdar-Shah, affordable innovation is about creating successful and sustainable businesses that have a significant focus on diseases of the poor – a challenge that enterprises in the developed world have often failed to meet.

Ongoing approaches to advance innovations in health for the poor include product-development public-private partnerships (PD-PPPs), advance market commitments, priority review vouchers, and patent pools to share intellectual property. Experience with PD-PPPs has shown that it is possible to develop complex innovative vaccines or medicines through a virtual and collaborative model.[21] Today, approximately 40 per cent of R&D expenditure for neglected tropical diseases comes from public-private partnerships[22] that rely on funding from the public, philanthropic, and private sectors. Products that have been developed using this strategy include anti-malarial drug formulation ASMQ (a combination drug including artesunate and mefloquine produced by Drugs for Neglected Diseases Initiative [DNDi]) and a new meningitis vaccine for an Africa-specific strain, (resulting from collaborative work of Program for Appropriate Technology in Health [PATH] and the Serum Institute of India). These efforts benefited from the participation of researchers and companies in the emerging markets of Brazil and India. Overall, however, our research suggests that the rising innovation capabilities of key emerging markets such as China, India, and Brazil, while constituting an important resource for addressing global health challenges, still remain largely untapped. Investment in firms in emerging markets represents a promising and innovative way in which development finance may be better used, as is underlined in a later chapter on development assistance by Janice Stein.

Discussion

The challenge of addressing global health is daunting in its magnitude. To be sure, enhancing access to health technologies is not just a supply-side issue; there are many reasons why available technologies often do not make it to the poor who desperately need them. However, particularly in the case of the two dozen or so neglected diseases that disproportionately affect the global poor, ensuring the availability of appropriate solutions remains a necessary first step in addressing their health needs. Any reduction in the development costs for such solutions should, in principle, lead to improved access, both by enhancing the ability of innovators to offer them at lower prices and by increasing the number of innovators.

Rising innovation capacity in key emerging markets such as China, India, South Korea, Brazil, South Africa, Taiwan, and other countries – both independently and in collaboration with actors in the industrialized world – holds tremendous potential for treating and/or preventing the diseases of poverty. What I have proposed here is in effect an attempt to link industry evolution to opportunities for value generation in addressing global health challenges. Similarly, an effective strategy for meeting the health technology needs of the developing world might be to marry "innovation *for* the South" to "innovation *with* the South." Involving increasingly capable emerging market entrepreneurs in innovation pursuits from the outset could improve cost effectiveness, enhance eventual market access, and ensure that end products are more appropriate for use in the developing world. The next chapter in this volume proposes a systematic way in which such collaborations might work.

Nevertheless, although a general shift towards value chain disaggregation is apparent, the direction in which the industry will evolve remains uncertain. Further work is required to identify viable entry and exit points within global value chains that would allow individual firms and countries to harvest value. In recent decades we have seen how information and telecommunication industries generate complex and innovative technologies through globalized and disaggregated value chains. The biopharmaceutical sector needs to study their example to find ways to reduce innovation costs and enhance therapeutic choice for the poor.

In this chapter I have argued that (a) the global biopharmaceutical innovation enterprise is becoming increasingly disaggregated, with a consequent increase of innovation capability in emerging markets; (b) the resultant distributed innovation value chain lends itself to more cost-effective innovations, in part by facilitating Southern innovation and entrepreneurship; (c) the globalization of innovation presents emerging and developing nations with new opportunities for economic development by tapping into global innovation value chains; and (d) while a disaggregated innovation chain can facilitate innovations that address the needs of the poor, at least in the case of neglected diseases, this will not happen automatically but will require the coordinated engagement of various stakeholders. Further economic and institutional support for scientists and innovators in settings of poverty has the potential to unleash powerful forces that will advance innovation and the scaling up of solutions.

Innovating for the poor, therefore, is more about innovating *with* and *by* actors in settings of poverty rather than *for* them. As former U.S.

president Bill Clinton has said, "Intelligence and effort are evenly distributed throughout the world, but opportunity and systems are not." A distributed innovation system with components in the developing world can enhance the ability of local stakeholders to direct their intelligence and efforts towards finding solutions to meet their own needs. However, the complexity and scale of global health challenges demand that we also pool our collective knowledge of appropriate technology (chapter 2), consumer psychology (chapter 3), strategies for innovation and scaling up (chapters 5 and 6), financial sources and models (chapters 7 and 8), and industry and globalization dynamics.

THE IDEA IN BRIEF

Rising scientific and technological capabilities in key emerging markets and a number of newly industrialized economies – together with other factors – have enabled the globalization and disaggregation of innovation activity in the biopharmaceutical sector. The resultant industry structure is more amenable to pro-poor innovations, in part by allowing for greater participation of low- and middle-income countries in the innovation process.

IMPLICATIONS

1   A disaggregated value chain allows for inclusive innovation, where actors and institutions in proximal settings of poverty participate in innovation and, through the process of learning-by- doing, enhance prospects for future engagement in both collaborative and independent innovation.
2   The engagement of scientists and innovators in proximal settings of poverty makes it more likely that resultant solutions will be more appropriate and affordable, while bringing state-of-the- art knowledge and technologies to address the needs of the poor.
3   Value chain disaggregation lowers entry barriers for new firms, regions, and countries, enabling them to participate in niche segments and reap economic and social benefits.

FOOD FOR THOUGHT

The diffusion of biopharmaceutical innovation activity in emerging markets – particularly China and India – may have short-term adverse economic effects for incumbent innovating nations such as the United States, the United Kingdom, Germany, France, and others. Can we make the case that it is in the interest of the latter group of countries to support the building of health innovation capacity in the former?

REFERENCES

1 Rezaie, A., McGahan, A.M., Daar, A., & Singer, P.A. (2012). "Innovative drugs and vaccines in China, India and Brazil." *Nature Biotechnology* 30: 10.

2 Mytelka, L.K. (2006). "Pathways and policies to (bio) pharmaceutical innovation systems in developing countries." *Industry and Innovation* 13 (4): 415–35.

3 Nóbrega O. de T., Marques, A., de Araújo, A., Karnikowski, M., Naves Jde, O., & LD, S. (2007). "Retail prices of essential drugs in Brazil: An international comparison." *Rev Panam Salud Publica*, 22 (2): 118–23.

4 Daar, A., Singer, P., Persad, D., Pramming, S., Matthews, D., Beaglehole, R., & Ganguly, N. (2007). "Grand challenges in chronic non-communicable diseases." *Nature* 450 (7169): 494–6.

5 Scully, T. (2012). "Diabetes in numbers." *Nature* 485 (7398): S2–S3; and UNESCO. (2010). *Unesco science report.*

6 DiMasi, J., Hansen, R., & Grabowski, H. (2003). "The price of innovation: New estimates of drug development costs." *Journal of Health Economics* 22 (2): 151–85; and DiMasi, J.A., & Grabowski, H.G. (2007). "The cost of biopharmaceutical R&D: Is biotech different?" *Managerial and Decision Economics* 28: 469–79.

7 Kyle, M.K., & McGahan, A.M. (2012). "Investments in pharmaceuticals before and after TRIPS." *Review of Economics and Statistics* (MIT Press) 94 (4): 1157–72.

8 Hafner, T., & Popp, D. (2011). *China and India as suppliers of affordable medicines to developing countries.* NBER Working Paper Series. Cambridge, MA: National Bureau of Economic Research.

9 The Access to Medicine Index 2012. Retrieved from: http://www .accesstomedicineindex.org/sites/www.accesstomedicineindex.org/files /2012-access-to-medicine-index-clickable.pdf.

10 Henderson, R., Orsenigo, L., & Pisano, G. (1999). "The pharmaceutical industry and the revolution in molecular biology: Interactions among scientific, institutional and organizational change." In D. Mowery & R. Nelson (Eds), *Sources of industrial leadership: Studies of seven industries,* 267–311. Cambridge: Cambridge University Press.

11 Hill, R., & Chui, M. (2009). "The pharmerging future." *Pharmaceutical Executive Magazine* 29 (7). Retrieved from: http://www.imshealth.com/imshealth

/Global/Content/Document/Intelligence.360%20Documents/The_Phar-merging_Future.pdf.

12 Howells, J., Gagliardi, D., & Malik, K. (2008). "The growth and manage-ment of R&D outsourcing: Evidence from UK pharmaceuticals." *R&D Management* 38 (2): 205–19.

13 Arora, A., & Gambardella, A. (1990). "Complementarity and external link-ages: The strategies of the large firms in biotechnology." *The Journal of In-dustrial Economics* 37 (4) (June): 361–79; and Rothaermel, F.T., & Hess, A.M. (2007). "Building dynamic capabilities: Innovation driven by individual-, firm-, and network-level effects." *Organization Science* 18 (6): 898–921.

14 Patel, P., & Pavitt, K. (1991). "Large firms in the production of the world's technology – an important case of non globalization." *Journal of Internation-al Business Studies* 22 (1): 1–21; Pavitt, K. (2001). "Managing global innova-tion: Uncovering the secrets of future competitiveness." *Research Policy* 30 (1): 176–7; Pavitt, K. (2002). "The globalizing learning economy." *Acad-emy of Management Review* 27 (1): 125–7; and Pavitt, K., & Patel, P. (1999). "Global corporations and national systems of innovation: Who dominates whom?" In D. Archibugi, J. Howells, & J. Michie (Eds), *Innovation policy in a global economy*, 94–119. Cambridge: Cambridge University Press.

15 Al-Bader, S., Frew, S.E., & Essajee, I. (2009). "Small but tenacious: South Africa's health biotech sector." *Nature Biotechnology* 27 (5): 427–45; Rezaie, R., Frew, S.E., Sammut, S.M., Maliakkal, M.R., Daar, A.S., & Singer, P.A. (2008). "Brazilian health biotech – fostering crosstalk between public and private sectors." *Nature Biotechnology* 26 (6); 627–44; Frew, S.E., Sammut, S.M., Shore, A.F., Ramjist, J.K., Al-Bader, S., Rezaie, R., et al. (2008). "Chi-nese health biotech and the billion-patient market: Chinese government support and 'sea turtles' are spurring the sector, but investors lack exits." *Nature Biotechnology* 26 (1): 37–54; and Rezaie, R., McGahan, A.M., Frew, S.E., Daar, A.S., & Singer, P.A. (2012). "Emergence of biopharmaceutical innovators in China, India, Brazil, and South Africa as global competitors and collaborators." *Health Research Policy and Systems* 10 (1): 18.

16 Rezaie, A., McGahan, A.M., Daar, A., & Singer, P.A. (2012). "Innovative drugs and vaccines in China, India and Brazil." *Nature Biotechnology* 30: 10; and Rezaie, R., & Singer, P.A. (2010). "Global health or global wealth?" *Nature Biotechnology* 28 (9), 907–9.

17 Armisted, L. (2012). "Drugs giant Novartis warns jobs may go overseas." *The Telegraph* (26 November). Retrieved 15 December 2012 from: http://www.telegraph.co.uk/finance/newsbysector/pharmaceuticalsandchemicals/9702054/Drugs-giant-Novartis-warns-jobs-may-go-overseas.html.

18 Cooper, R. (2011). "Pfizer to close Viagra research site, putting 2,400 UK jobs at risk." *The Telegraph* (1 February). "Retrieved 15 December 2012 from: http://www.telegraph.co.uk/finance/newsbysector/pharmaceuticalsandchemicals/8296725/Pfizer-to-close-Viagra-research-site-putting-2400-UK-jobs-at-risk.html.

19 "GSK to cut 90 jobs." (2012). *Pharmacy News* (28 November). Retrieved 15 December 2012 from: http://www.pharmacynews.com.au/news/latest-news/gsk-to-cut-90-jobs.

20 Daar, A., & Singer, P. (2011). *The grandest challenge: Taking life-saving science from lab to village*. Toronto: Doubleday Canada.

21 Nwaka, S., & Ridley, R.G. (2003). "Virtual drug discovery and development for neglected diseases through public-private partnerships." *Nature Reviews Drug Discovery* 2 (11): 919–28.

22 The Access to Medicine Index 2012. Retrieved from: http://www.accesstomedicineindex.org/sites/www.accesstomedicineindex.org/files/2012-access-to-medicine-index-clickable.pdf.

5

Embedded Innovation in Health

ANITA M. McGAHAN
RAHIM REZAIE
DONALD C. COLE

Interest in innovative technologies for improving the health of the poor has never been greater. In the 2001 Human Development Report, Mark Malloch-Brown, a key architect of the United Nations Millennium Development Goals, spoke of "the explosion of technological innovation in food, medicine and information ... that, if harnessed effectively, could transform the lives of poor people and offer breakthrough development opportunities to poor countries."[1] Stephen A. Matlin, then executive director of Global Forum for Health Research (based in Switzerland), noted in 2008 that "the Global Forum for Health Research ... seeks to promote innovation in all fields that will improve the health of poor populations and reduce health inequities."[2] In a November 2011 report to the G20 entitled "Innovating with Impact: Financing 21st Century Development," Bill Gates wrote, "The capacity to innovate is spreading beyond the richest countries into a larger set of rapidly growing economies ... [I]nnovation is the most powerful force for change in the world."[3] The principal recommendation of the report was to invite the G20 to identify a list of high-priority innovations for development – similar to the Millennium Development Goals – for focusing and coordinating effort.

Several excellent recent analyses have pointed to the fact that innovation in the Global South has the potential not just to improve the lives of the poor but also to improve the lives of the wealthy. In chapter 4 of this volume, Rahim Rezaie demonstrates how biopharmaceutical companies in middle-income countries have responded to opportunities for innovation in a way that both benefits local patients and serves as a potential foundation for global competitive and comparative advantage. Other analyses emphasize the equally important challenge of lowering the costs of health-care delivery in relatively wealthy countries to enhance sustainability and in relatively poor countries to enhance accessibility. The World Health Organization's (WHO) Global Health Expenditure Atlas published in 2012 indicates that the United States spends $8,362 per person per year on health care,[4] an unsustainable figure even in that wealthy country. Other major industrialized nations such as Canada, the United Kingdom, France, and Germany are also struggling with rising health-care costs. Innovation to reduce costs while improving quality in health-care delivery is thus imperative. In poor countries, where per-capita gross domestic product (GDP) is often below the per-capita health expenditure for countries in the Organization for Economic Co-operation and Development (OECD), the possibility of closing the gap in health-care systems with the high-income countries is remote under current conditions. Innovation in the Global South to lower the costs of essential health-care technologies and processes has the potential to improve welfare globally, as well as permit expansion of coverage to the excluded.[5]

In this chapter, we build on Cheng and Bradley's chapter 3 in this volume, "Appropriate Technologies for the Global South," to review current thinking on innovation aimed at improving the health of the global poor. We observe that much of the discourse surrounding innovation, although well-intentioned, is motivated by concerns that are more relevant to high-income than to low-income countries. These apprehensions arise from several factors: concerns on the part of companies in high-income countries that innovations in the low- and middle-income countries (LMICs) could have adverse competitive implications for them; ongoing cost crises in the health sector in the United States and other high-income countries; and, more broadly, ongoing uncertainties related to the financial crisis of 2008 and its continuing repercussions. As such, we are concerned that frameworks that promise cost-conscious innovations, although in some cases emerging out of LMICs themselves (particularly from India), may be used as instruments to advance rich country interests without sufficient benefits to the poor in low- and middle-income nations. We are also concerned that the prevalent discourse on innovation, particularly that aimed at advancing innovation for the poor, inadvertently creates different standards for the rich versus the poor. In response, we propose a framework we call embedded innovation in health (EIH), which puts the health needs and livelihood interests of the global poor at the centre of the innovation agenda, engages them in the process, and is more likely to enhance equity in health, economic, and social terms.

Innovation Concepts

Most innovation programs are built on the assumptions of affluence and abundance … However, we see shaken consumers in the United States and Europe asking for inexpensive or value-for-money products and services. We see billions of first-time consumers in China and India – where economic growth is surging and 2 billion to 3 billion people will join the middle class in the next decade – who can afford only the cheapest offerings. We see the rich and the young in both the developed and the developing worlds demanding environment-friendly products and services. Affordability and sustainability, not premium pricing and abundance, should drive innovation today.[6]

Developing countries are becoming hotbeds of business innovation in much the same way as Japan did from the 1950s onwards. They are coming up with new products and services that are dramatically cheaper than their Western equivalents: $3,000 cars, $300 computers and $30 mobile phones that provide nationwide service for just 2 cents a minute. They are reinventing systems of production and distribution, and they are experimenting with entirely new business models. All the elements of modern business, from supply-chain management to recruitment and retention, are being re-jigged or reinvented in one emerging market or another.[7]

The preceding quotations highlight the changing realities in and perceptions of emerging markets. These changes stem both from the Western interest in exploring new ways of remaining competitive, in part by reaching new markets,[8] and from growing efforts to address poor-market needs through innovation. One consequence has been a considerable effort to understand and promote cost-effective innovations to improve the livelihood of millions of people in LMICs, sometimes with the goal of "importing" the resultant innovations to high-income countries. The resulting discourse on cost-effective innovations has given birth to a number of concepts used by scholars and practitioners to model innovations by, for, and with the poor in LMIC settings.

Here we discuss some of the major concepts and examine their relevance and limitations from the perspective of both innovators and eventual end users. The various concepts are not mutually exclusive, and there are no sharp distinctions between them. We have summarized key aspects of each to highlight the richness of the ideas, and also to elucidate areas for development. Furthermore, we have limited this exercise to the terms that we feel are most commonly used in discussing innovations that may originate in low- and middle-income countries and also have application in high-income nations. In the interests of space and focus, we do not describe related terms such as "constraint-based innovation," "grassroots innovation," and "user-centred innovation," despite their value and relevance to broad innovation processes (see the glossary for definitions of these terms).

Appropriate Technology

The concept of appropriate technology has a long history. It also has closely related antecedents in ideas such as low-cost and intermediate technologies. The concept of "intermediate technology" is attributed to Dr Ernst Friedrich Schumacher, who, in his influential 1973 book, *Small Is Beautiful: Economics as if People Mattered*,[9] suggested that small, appropriate technologies are more empowering than industrial technologies. Mahatma Gandhi was also a strong advocate for the utilization of affordable, locally relevant technologies that could help villages achieve self-reliance. The concept has since acquired additional meanings and currently is associated with energy sustainability in the West and with inexpensive health products and services in LMICs. Examples of so-called appropriate technologies in such settings include pedal-powered water pumps, solar-powered light bulbs, and the Life Straw used to render unsanitary water potable. In global health, the Program for Appropriate Technologies in Health (www.path.org) is known for developing high-quality appropriate technologies such as portable diagnostics, vaccines for meningitis, and protocols for the prevention of diarrheal disease (see Cheng and Bradley's discussion in chapter 3 of this volume for examples).

At its core, the appropriate technologies concept in LMICs reflects the idea that some technologies that work in high-income countries do not work in the former because of important contextual differences such as the variability of electricity supplies, the uncertain availability of spare parts, and the need for special tolerances related to temperature fluctuations. The idea has also been criticized for justifying low-quality outcomes in low- and middle-income countries that would not be acceptable in the industrialized nations. The concept deals with the demand side of innovations but does not address how such technologies are developed in the first place. Furthermore, most conceptions of appropriate technology qualify innovations on criteria such as relative cost, engineering sophistication, and sustainability, broadly defined. Therefore, the character of "appropriateness" is fluid, context specific, and disease specific.

Frugal Innovation

In attempting to theorize on frugal innovation, Bhatti (2012)[10] concludes that it lies at the intersection of technological, institutional, and social innovation. The logic of "frugal innovation" in health care has garnered attention as a way to improve the living conditions of people in LMICs. Common examples of frugal innovation are the Aakash Tablet, the Tata Nano, One Laptop Per Child, and individually packed shampoo sachets, which were highlighted in C.K. Prahalad's *The Fortune at the Bottom of the Pyramid.*[11] Many of these innovations originated in India or were inspired by the Indian context. Both government and industry in India have adopted frugal innovation as a viable approach to enhancing the country's social and economic well-being. As Shashi Tharoor, a member of the Indian Parliament writes, "India's leadership in 'frugal innovation' goes beyond downsizing: it involves starting with the needs of poor consumers … and working backwards. Instead of complicating or refining their products, Indian innovators strip them down to their bare essentials, making them affordable, accessible, durable and effective."[12] Indian biotechnology companies Biocon (Bangalore) and Shantha Biotecnics (Hyderabad) have adopted the frugal innovation mindset by improving manufacturing processes to drastically reduce the price of insulin (a treatment for diabetes) and the hepatitis B vaccine.[13] The mindset is not confined to India. Indigenous biopharmaceutical entrepreneurs in China, Cuba, India, and Brazil have engaged in innovations that preferentially tackle local diseases, in part by engaging in less resource-intensive innovation activities.[14] Frugal innovation has also been embraced by firms in high-income countries as a mechanism for both lowering the costs of the innovation process and reducing the complexity of end products.[15]

Reverse Innovation

Govindarajan and colleagues[16] have elucidated the concept of "reverse innovation," which describes how organizations benefit from products, processes, and ideas that are first commercialized in low- and middle-income countries and subsequently in high-income countries. The idea of "reverse" denotes this model's emphasis on the direction that innovations flow; namely from low- to high-income countries rather than the reverse, which is more common. Processes of reverse innovation resist the common practice of modifying existing products to fit the demands of users in developing countries. Govindarajan and Trimble (2011)[17] explain that, given the qualitatively different nature of LMIC markets and the price-sensitivity of consumers, innovative products and processes must be designed expressly for these settings. At the core of the "reverse innovation" idea is an emphasis on the ultimate relevance of such innovations for high-income countries. The link is via the concept of disruption. Because global multinational corporations increasingly face competition from firms based in the developing world, their survival and competitiveness depend on early access to low-cost innovations that may disrupt current approaches. The prescription for global multinationals is to develop new products, business models, and strategies to suit low- and middle-income countries' specifications and to hold an option on introducing the innovations in core markets in high-income countries. A key premise of this model is the heuristic that LMIC consumers will accept, say, a 50 per cent solution, so long as they pay only 15 per cent of the price relative to high-income countries.

Jugaad Innovation

Radjou, Prabhu, and Ahuja (2011)[18] describe *"jugaad"* as characteristic of innovation processes in India and other resource-constrained settings. *Jugaad*, which the authors translate as "an innovative fix; an improvised solution born from ingenuity and cleverness," signifies innovation in the face of resource constraints. The process of *jugaad* innovation can lead to elegant, resilient, and low-cost approaches for addressing compelling, genuine, and immediate challenges. The authors offer examples such as Mitticool, a "fridge" made of clay that does not require electricity, inspired by the modern refrigerator but designed to use available materials and to accommodate the electricity constraints typical of LMIC markets. The authors also observe that *"Jugaad* is currently the dominant form of innovation in emerging markets ... [as it] was once a big part of Western innovation too."[19] They cite U.S. inventions such as the mechanical grain reaper developed by Cyrus McCormick and his son in 1831, and a number of inventions by Benjamin Franklin, such as a more efficient stove, the lightning rod, bifocals, and a carriage odometer. But over time, they argue, high-income countries lost *jugaad* as R&D activities became institutionalized and thus encumbered by rigidities and unsustainable cost structures. The prescription, some argue, is for firms in high-income countries to return to the simplicity, flexibility, and frugality of the *jugaad* mindset in order to become more innovative in an increasingly competitive world. A central facet of the *jugaad* approach is an emphasis on the innovation process, which involves elements of both planning and experimentation. In that regard, some *jugaad* innovations are not qualitatively different from those customary in the West that rely substantially on experimentation with available materials, which the French have embraced as "bricolage."

Radjou and colleagues are not alone in seeing potential in Eastern approaches to shape Western thinking and business strategies. Kumar and Puranam (2011)[20] develop the idea that uniquely Indian ways of thinking may lead to technological breakthroughs in platform technologies with the potential for disrupting the cost structures of products and services in a range of industries, including health care. Constantinos Markides of the London Business School sees disruptions from the so-called "bottom of the pyramid" as carrying the potential to challenge the structures of global industries in a fundamental way.[21]

Inclusive Innovation

George, McGahan, and Prabhu (2012) define inclusive innovation as "the development and implementation of new ideas which aspire to create opportunities that enhance social and economic well-being for disenfranchised members of society."[22] This concept, which has become central to public policy in India, advocates the application of sophisticated engineering and design capabilities in products and services that benefit lower-income consumers and that simultaneously enrich lower-income entrepreneurs. The goal of inclusive innovation is the enhanced social and economic well-being of disenfranchised populations. The inclusive innovation construct stresses the "removal of economic, geographic, social, and other structural barriers that previously blocked access to opportunity" and values efforts to enhance access to opportunity independently of whether these efforts are ultimately successful in achieving their goals. The ultimate goal of inclusive innovation, the authors argue, is an equitable distribution of opportunity within a given society. They consider practices such as fair trade, distance learning, and restorative justice as examples.

Canada's International Development Research Centre (IDRC) promotes a similar concept, Innovation for Inclusive Development (IID).[23] Recognizing the persistence of the highly inequitable distribution of innovation benefits, this program supports work that examines how innovations within informal sectors can influence the well-being of poor citizens. Conceptually, IID and inclusive innovation as a concept share a focus on enhancing access to resources and opportunity for the poor (in keeping with Wong's argument in chapter 1 of this volume).

Integrated Innovation

In the business and management literature, the notion of integrated innovation denotes coordinated activities either within different functional units of a given firm or across a supply chain.[24] For example, a firm espousing a vertically integrated innovation model would in effect internalize the various capabilities required for a specific set of innovations and coordinate various functional units' activities towards the goal of developing novel products or technologies.

In the context of addressing global health challenges, Grand Challenges Canada defines integrated innovation as

> the coordinated application of scientific/technological, social and business innovation to develop solutions to complex challenges. This approach does not discount the singular benefits of each of these types of innovation alone, but rather highlights the powerful synergies that can be realized by aligning all three. Integrated Innovation recognizes that scientific/technological innovations have a greater chance of going to scale and achieving global impact and sustainability if they are developed from the outset with appropriate social and business innovations.[25]

Thus, integrated innovation stems from the recognition that, to solve complex challenges such as the health needs of the global poor, innovation must occur simultaneously in multiple arenas.

Why Are We Concerned?

We share optimism that low-cost technologies originating in resource-limited settings have the potential to change the structure of health delivery not only in low- and middle-income countries but also in high-income nations. Important medical devices, pharmaceuticals, and service delivery protocols have already originated in settings of poverty and reshaped the landscape for heath practice in particular fields. These include the Jaipur foot, an early "appropriate" technology celebrated by C.K. Prahalad in his book *The Fortune at the Bottom of the Pyramid*;[26] generic versions of highly active anti-retroviral medicines for treating human immunodeficiency virus (HIV) infections; affordable eye care and eye surgery by India's Aravind hospital network (see chapter 1 in this volume); and community-health models for assuring patient adherence to complex home-therapy regimens.

A concern that arises regarding the potential for South-to-North innovation, and particularly with the implementation of the innovation concepts profiled here, is that these approaches carry the potential to exacerbate governance paradoxes and maintain or exacerbate health inequities. This may occur, for example, by encouraging the off-shoring of risky projects to places where vulnerable patients may participate in the innovation process but not accrue rights over the technologies that emerge from their participation. For example, when clinical trials on new drugs are organized in settings of poverty that lack adequate institutional safeguards, the risk of failure may be localized in a community of vulnerable patients, but the benefits of success may not be fully localized in the same community.

Another question relates to the applicability of approaches such as *jugaad* and frugal innovation to complex and knowledge-intensive innovations – for instance, innovations required to develop safe and efficacious vaccines and medicines for diseases that disproportionately afflict people in settings of poverty. These technologies often require that we bring to bear our best and most current understanding of disease processes. It is not clear that *jugaad* and frugal innovation approaches can help us get there by pooling our collective global resources, including knowledge, to solve major global health challenges. The reverse innovation approach on the other hand draws on global expertise but sacrifices substantial performance in exchange for a very low price. In the context of health products and services, most would find this approach morally objectionable. How can we accept a vaccine or medicine that works 50 per cent of the time and/or has an inferior safety profile for use in low- and middle-income countries while a much more superior solution is available elsewhere?

Unfortunately, regarding the above-mentioned approaches as the primary mode of innovation for the global poor increases the likelihood that these populations will receive a different class of products and services – one that is characterized by lower quality, albeit at a lower price. The real question ought to be: How do we enhance access to state-of-the-art health and other technologies and services at an affordable price? A fridge made of clay that does not require electricity and operates in temperate climates can be considered at best a stop-gap, temporary measure. These innovations offer substantial value but are far from permanent solutions.

To the extent that the innovation concepts discussed above are focused on simplifying existing approaches or technologies to arrive at more affordable alternatives, they are tantamount to a "technology-push" strategy. In other words, they are attempts to find new uses or markets for existing solutions. In technological terms this often translates into making Western technologies more accessible to LMICs. We concur with Govindarajan and Trimble[27] that while such innovations offer considerable scope to improve the livelihoods of millions in low- and middle-income countries, they are unlikely to reach the mass market in these settings without a radical redesign that drastically reduces the price consumers must pay. From the perspective of enhancing access for poor populations in poor markets, however, even if a multinational reduces the cost of a health product or service from $5,000 to $2,500, the reduction is unlikely to make much of a dent. The key point is that these solutions were not developed in the first instance with the poor market as their primary target, nor was scale-up designed with bottom-up as well as top-down approaches (see chapter 6 in this volume). What we need is an approach that at its very core aims at innovating for the poor and, in the process, accounts for contextual nuances that affect the poor. Supporting innovation capabilities in settings of poverty can help us make progress towards achieving this objective.

Embedded Innovation

We propose an alternative framework that aims to advance health innovations for the poor while safeguarding both their short-term and their long-term social and economic interests. This approach, which we call embedded innovation,[28] offers the potential to break the impasse on disruptive health innovation. It builds on ideas elaborated in the business literature[29] and aims for inclusive innovation for growth[30] and development.[31]

Embedded innovation for health (EIH) is guided by several core principles. First, embedded innovation is based on a commitment to solidarity with the poor, genuine concern over their welfare, and accounting for the distributive consequences of innovation by ensuring adequate access to and/or ownership of the resulting solutions. Second, it treats the poor as the primary market during the entire innovation process. Third, the innovation process starts with a deep understanding of contextual nuances and involves patients and care providers in the settings where the eventual solutions are to be applied. We use the notion of embeddedness to highlight the inseparability of the first three principles in working to meet specific needs of poor populations in particular contexts. The fourth principle of embedded innovation is that, though embedded in a local context, it must draw on state-of-the-art knowledge and technologies to arrive at the best, highest-quality solutions to health challenges. In this respect it does not compromise on the safety and efficacy of health interventions. The Cuban experience with health bio-technology development in a resource-constrained context is particularly instructive and relevant to this fourth principle.[32]

Ansari and colleagues[33] argue that inclusive innovation is most successful when the innovation process is embedded within the social context of poor communities. Embeddedness within the social context, they argue, can provide the necessary social capital to help innovators avoid negative social consequences. Bradley and colleagues[34] find that innovation mediates the association between various forms of capital (including financial, social, and human capital), and suggest that all three forms of capital are required to enhance living conditions in resource-constrained settings. In the context of inclusive entrepreneurship, Hall and colleagues[35] find that public policies that are more in line with the cultural and institutional dimensions of a society are more likely to generate productive outcomes and enhance social inclusion.

To elaborate on the notions mentioned above, EIH has the following characteristics:

Collaboration in the Field

Just as Muhammad Yunus spent time with villagers to come up with the Grameen banking model, innovators can become embedded in

communities in order to understand, through collaboration and solidarity, the vulnerabilities of poor people as citizens and patients as well as
the potential for affordable, high-quality advances. A historical example
is that of village health workers, a model developed through interaction
among policy leaders and community organizations as a way to improve
access to health care among the underserved.[36] Rezaie's chapter in this
volume (chapter 4) on the prospects of disaggregated innovation value
chains for advancing health technology innovation is in essence a way to
embed resource-intensive innovations in poverty settings through collaborative partnerships involving local firms and other actors and institutions. Examples of successful embedded innovation demonstrate the
following qualities:

- Immersion. In many resource-limited settings, patients cannot fully
  articulate needs and preferences in interviews. Restrictions on
  expression arise for a range of reasons that include lack of familiar-
  ity with what is possible as well as concerns about alienating the
  interviewer with demanding requirements. Analysis of the needs
  of users and the psychological dimensions that shape their decision
  making (as discussed by Dilip Soman in chapter 2 in this volume)
  requires immersion by the innovator in the situation of the patient
  and of the health-care provider.
- Contextual relevance. At the heart of embedded innovation is the
  idea that the technology will improve patient health in the context
  in which it is developed. The innovation is designed specifically for
  the situation of the patient on which the technology is tested – not
  simply to achieve lower costs elsewhere.
- Use-based analysis. The design principles behind embedded innovation emphasize intensive analysis of the use case among citizens,
  patients, and health providers. Innovation arises through solidarity
  with citizens and patients on their terms.

Risk and Profit Sharing.

Innovations that generate extensive margins of profit normally also
generate extensive margins of risk. These risks may be absorbed in due
course in relatively wealthier contexts where the consequences are
primarily financial but not personally devastating. In poor countries,
where rules of law and normal practice may not be adequate to protect
innovators or the vulnerable, the imposition of these risks may lead
to devastating consequences for patients and communities. Thus, the

innovation process must deal sensitively with the risk-sharing as well as the profit-sharing consequences of innovation.

Minimal Reliance on Competition in Experimental Processes and Maximal Reliance on Competition to Serve the Poor

Current gold standards for health effectiveness involve randomized controlled trials and other mechanisms for experimentation that frequently place the burden of failed health innovations on less informed and more vulnerable patients.[37] Embedded innovation involves minimal reliance on experiments in the initial stages, with a full exploration of the distribution of their consequences so as to minimize adverse impacts on poor patients. The following considerations should apply:

- Experimental design. Experiments are designed to evaluate not only whether the intervention is effective but also which among the available innovations is the most effective.
- Experimental methods. Randomized treatments to test for efficacy are conducted only after extensive refinement of the technology, as is common in drug development in the industrialized world.
- Research ethics clearance. The design and conducting of experiments conform not to minimum local standards and regulations but to those of global best practices and key ethical principles, including justice, autonomy, beneficence, and non-maleficence. Such clearance is obtained even in situations, such as non-health interventions, where it is not required, given the interest in health outcomes.
- Theoretical frontier. The innovation represents the best available medical, scientific, and social knowledge *throughout* the innovation process. This means that revisions are implemented and the experimentation process is reconstituted, if necessary, if breakthroughs occur after initiation.
- Timetable. The intervention process proceeds according to a timetable that is developed based on inputs from the full range of stakeholders, not just those of the innovators or investors. The needs and circumstances of the community, citizens, and patients are respected.

In addition, there should be a balanced emphasis on prevention and early diagnosis as well as on treatment. The Holy Grail in health is prevention, with early diagnosis of many medical conditions and the specialized treatment of patients with complex and acute conditions as complementary to prevention. Achieving a balance of investments across these activities – prevention, diagnosis, and treatment – is challenging even in wealthier countries. Allocating resources for innovation should respect this balance rather than only translate affordable, high-quality treatments among rich and poor both within and across countries.

Potential Drawbacks and Limitations of EIH

While we believe that the EIH framework, as we have laid it out, would serve to advance innovation for the poor in a more just and ethical fashion, we are concerned about the unintended consequences of deliberate, planned interventions that seek to capture the creative potential of resource-constrained innovators.[38] The field of global health is fraught with paradoxes that give rise to differences across geographies in the availability and cost of health-restoring technologies. McGahan[39] describes paradoxes in mortality, technology, affordability, access, disruptive innovation, prevention, and treatment. The unifying characteristic of paradoxes in the field is that, without optimal governance, the very technologies that have the greatest potential to improve health can also centralize power, wealth, and control.[40] Centralization, in turn, is often associated with illness and inequality. For example, breakthrough medical devices and pharmaceuticals that are privately owned are typically only available in settings where prices are sufficiently high to support a return on the prior investment needed to create such innovations. Hum and colleagues[41] find evidence suggesting that the mechanisms that give rise to inequalities may be subtle and unexpected: for instance, improvements in child health are accompanied by declines in adult health.

These and other paradoxical outcomes associated with the introduction of health technologies generally arise from governance challenges. Governance over any intervention involves the allocation of property, decision, and control rights.[42] Health technologies are particularly vulnerable to paradox because the property rights that arise from invention are normally allocated to the inventor, while the value of the technology is obtained only through the restoration of human health, which is, under prevalent norms, under the control and decision authority of patient advocates (such as physicians) and patients.

Inaction in the face of health crises is intolerable. All action, including even the promotion of a concept such as EIH, leads to unintended consequences that must be managed carefully. EIH reflects the challenge of integrating humanitarian action with state-of-the-art approaches to innovation.

THE IDEA IN BRIEF

Without adequate safeguards, the prevalent discourse on ways to advance innovations for the global poor risks creating different standards for rich and poor. In the context of health products and services in particular, we find this prospect highly objectionable on ethical grounds. As a result, we have proposed a new framework we call embedded innovation in health, which we believe places the poor at the centre of the innovation agenda and is more likely to be equity enhancing.

DISCUSSION

Tension arises in the relationship between embedded innovation and scaling. Taken to the extreme, "embedded" innovation involves tailoring a technological approach to context, whereas scaling involves taking advantage of the platform created by technology to improve the access to and the affordability and quality of useful, prosperity-enhancing activities. Resolving this tension requires thinking about innovation as a complex, process-bound set of activities, capabilities, and resources rather than a monolithic technology. Just as embedded journalists in military action document the connections between scaled action and local impact, embedded innovators in the war against poverty may document the connections between the scale afforded by the technology or other interventions and the contextual requirements of the communities in which technologies are introduced. The ultimate goal is to develop a set of balanced principles that assure that the process of developing and introducing an innovative solution does not ultimately exploit the poor by siphoning a disproportionate share of the economic, cultural, and political benefits to resource-rich actors. Balance in the implementation of a platform to achieve both the benefits of scale and local relevance is critical to the success of efforts to alleviate poverty and improve prosperity for all engaged stakeholders.

This chapter connects to others in this volume in several ways. In chapter 3, Cheng and Bradley describe in detail how appropriate technologies achieve precisely the balance between scale and relevance that is at the core of embedded innovation. The loss of value associated with the failed introduction of inappropriate technologies, such as discarded walkers outside a hospital in The Gambia or the PlayPumps set up in a number of African countries, points to the multiple levels at which a failure to embed local context and understanding in the innovation process may arise. It suggests that embeddedness is necessary in every activity, from problem definition to the selection of the technology to its design and implementation. In chapter 2, Soman outlines the challenges of demonstrating the relevance of technology as part of the implementation process. Effective marketing is, essentially, embedding the relevance of the benefits of a technology in the presentation to consumers. In chapter 8, Stein points to the centrality of this relevance to public policy, especially as public actors seek to eliminate waste and advance collaboration between public and private actors in resource-rich and resource-limited settings.

The tight relationships between adaptability, embeddedness, and innovation point to the centrality of governance in the introduction of technologies into resource-limited settings. The literature has established that the inclusion of a wide variety of stakeholders is crucial to the success of innovation. The analysis that we have presented in this paper highlights that effective, enfranchising governance is central as well to the adaptability of innovation over time to retain relevance. Embedded governance is a core facet of effective innovation.

IMPLICATIONS

The concept of embedded innovation carries a number of implications for scholars, practitioners, and policymakers. Among academics, a literature on realist evaluation emphasizes the importance of analysis that considers the scalability of a particular innovation in light of diversity in local contexts to extract generalizable approaches. Our analysis points to various opportunities for scholars interested in considering the levels at which local diversity arises: in the needs analysis associated with technology development; in the generality of the platform; in the feedback loop between use and design; in the marketing of the technology for use; and in the decision processes that are used to govern both the adaptation of the technology over time and the distribution of rewards associated with the prosperity that an innovation enables. Each of these ideas requires substantial study.

"Embedded innovation" is also an important concept for practitioners. The field of innovation for the global poor is replete with stories, examples, and principles that reflect the hazards of introducing new approaches without full consideration of their implications for all stakeholders, and especially the poor. The recent introduction of concepts such as "reverse innovation," "*jugaad* innovation," and "frugal innovation" suggests the potential for value creation of technologies that are developed in and for the Global South. Our analysis points to the risks of pursuing these ideas without full consideration of their implications for the poor. From a practical perspective, program officers within NGOs and health-care providers should be encouraged to engage with potential innovators in local settings, to respond to their challenges, be open to them, and exercise creativity with others within resource constraints. Innovating firms and managers should be equally open to partnerships with communities and civil society organizations, and, ultimately, willing to work to scale up successful interventions that are generalizable to other contexts. In doing so, it is imperative for innovators to bring to bear state-of-the-art knowledge of the health conditions that they intend to address, and to ensure that they do not unjustifiably sacrifice the safety and efficacy of health interventions in search of an ultra-low price.

The concept of embedded innovation is also important for public policy in settings of poverty and beyond. As mentioned by Janice Stein in chapter 8, a considerable portion of the world's poor now reside in middle-income countries, including India and China. These countries have embarked on ambitious agendas to enhance their scientific and technological development. They have the opportunity to link these efforts from the outset to the unmet needs of large, economically impoverished populations and to engage them in the process. With regard to the public policy implications for developed economies, poverty alleviation efforts should be more closely linked to localized capacity building in settings of poverty in a way that engages communities in finding innovative solutions to their own challenges and empowers them to lead similar efforts in the future.

FOOD FOR THOUGHT

While we have discussed the concept of embedded innovation in the context of health innovations, we believe it to be applicable to other spheres as well. Indeed, at least implicitly, many of the chapters in this book suggest that a deep understanding of end-user contexts and the engagement of these users are important for innovation and scale-up (see, for example, Phillips and colleagues in chapter 6 in this volume). We have focused on health, in part because it is a field in which the potential adverse consequences of disembedded innovation are likely to be serious in terms of their potential for inflicting social and/or physical harm. However, we recognize that global health challenges often demand the scale-up of successful interventions, and as such we must continuously face the tension between contextualization and scale-up, and strive to strike a balance by innovating in the governance of initiatives that seek to improve the health and prosperity of the poor.

REFERENCES

 1 Human Development Report. (2001). *Making new technologies work for human development*. Oxford: Oxford University Press, iii. Retrieved 24 January 2013 from: http://hdr.undp.org/en/media/completenew1.pdf.
 2 Matlin, Stephen A. (2008). "The scope and potential of innovation for health and health equity." In "Fostering innovation for global health," *Global Update on Research for Health* 5.
 3 Gates, Bill. (2011). "Innovating with impact: Financing 21st century development." *Report to the G20 leaders*, Cannes Summit (November).
 4 World Health Organization (WHO). (2012). *WHO Global Health Expenditure Atlas*. Retrieved 20 November 2012 from: http://www.who.int/nha/atlas2.pdf.
 5 See the introduction to this volume: Joseph Wong and Dilip Soman, "Innovating for the Global South: Towards an inclusive agenda."
 6 Prahalad, C.K., & Mashelkar, R.A. (2010). "Innovation's Holy Grail." *Harvard Business Review* (July).
 7 Wooldridge, A. (2010). "Innovation in emerging markets." *The Economist* (Special Report) (15 April). Retrieved 24 January 2013 from: http://www.economist.com/node/15879369.
 8 See chapter 1 in this volume: Joseph Wong, "Poverty invisibility and innovation."
 9 Schumacher, E.F. (1973). *Small is beautiful*. London: Sphere.
10 Bhatti, Y.A. (2012). "What is frugal, what is innovation? Towards a theory of frugal innovation." Retrieved 24 January 2013 from: http://papers.ssrn.com/sol3/papers.cfm?abstract_id=2005910.
11 Prahalad, C.K. (2004). *The fortune at the bottom of the pyramid*. Philadelphia: Wharton School Publishing.
12 Tharoor, S. (2012). "India's hope lies in frugal innovation." *New Straits Times* (23 July). Retrieved 24 January 2013 from: http://www.nst.com.my/opinion/columnist/india-s-hope-lies-in-frugal-innovation-1.111326.
13 Frew, S.E., Rezaie, R., & Sammut, S.M. (2007). "India's health biotech sector at a crossroads." *Nature Biotechnology* 25 (4): 403–17.
14 Rezaie, R., McGahan, A.M., Daar, A.S., & Singer, P.A. (2012). "Innovative drugs and vaccines in China, India and Brazil." *Nature Biotechnology*

30 (10): 923–6. Retrieved 24 January 2013 from: http://www.nature.com/nbt/journal/v30/n10/full/nbt.2380.html; and Rezaie, R., & Singer, P.A. (2010). "Global health or global wealth?" *Nature Biotechnology* 28 (9): 907–9. Retrieved 24 January 2013 from: http://www.nature.com/nbt/journal/v28/n9/full/nbt0910-907.html.

15 Topol, E.J. (2011). "Medicine needs frugal innovation." *Technology Review.* Cambridge, MA: MIT. Retrieved 20 January 2013 from: http://www.technologyreview.com/news/426336/medicine-needs-frugal-innovation/page/2/.

16 Govindarajan, V., & Trimble, C. (2011). *Reverse innovation: Create far from home, win everywhere.* Boston: Harvard Business Review Press; and Govindarajan, V., & Ramamurti, R. (2011). "Reverse innovation, emerging markets, and global strategy." *Global Strategy Journal* 1 (3–4): 191–205.

17 Govindarajan & Trimble (2011), *Reverse innovation.*

18 Radjou, N., Prahbu, J.,& Ajuja, S. (2011). *Jugaad innovation.* San Francisco: Jossey-Bass.

19 Ibid., 5.

20 Kumar, N., & Puranam, P. (2012). *India inside: The emerging innovation challenge to the West.* Boston: Harvard Business Review Press.

21 Markides, C.C. (2012). "How disruptive will innovations from emerging markets be?" *Sloan Management Review* 54 (1), Reprint: 54120.

22 George, G., McGahan, A., & Prabhu, J. (2012). "Innovation for inclusive growth: Towards a theoretical framework and a research agenda." *Journal of Management Studies* 49 (4): 661–83.

23 International Development Research Centre (IDRC). (2012). Retrieved 20 November 2012 from: http://www.idrc.ca/EN/Programs/Science_and_Innovation/Innovation_for_Inclusive_Development/Pages.

24 Rothwell, R. (1992). "Developments towards the fifth generation model of innovation." *Technology Analysis & Strategic Management* 1 (4): 73–5. Retrieved 20 January 2013 from: http://www.tandfonline.com/doi/pdf/10.1080/09537329208524080#.UfwEbm08kys

25 Grand Challenges Canada. Retrieved 20 November 2012 from: http://www.grandchallenges.ca/integrated-innovation/.

26 Prahalad (2004), *The fortune at the bottom of the pyramid.*

27 Govindarajan & Trimble (2011), *Reverse innovation.*

28 This idea was first outlined in McGahan, A. (2012). "Paradoxes of innovation in health and their resolution in embedded innovation" *Munk Monitor* 2 (Fall): 14–17; and McGahan, A. (2012). "The new agenda for business schools: Creating problem solvers for the world." *Rotman Magazine* (Spring): 21–7.

29 Simanis, E., & Hart. S. (2009). "Innovation from the inside out." *MIT Sloan Management Review.* 50 (4), Reprint 50414.

30 George, McGahan, & Prabhu (2012), "Innovation for inclusive growth."

31 IDRC (2012). Retrieved 20 November 2012 from: http://www.idrc.ca /EN/Programs/Science_and_Innovation/Innovation_for_Inclusive _Development/Pages.

32 Thorsteinsdóttir, H., Saénz, T.W., Quach, U., Daar, A.S., & Singer, P.A. (2004). "Cuba – innovation through synergy." *Nature Biotechnology* 22 (Supplement): DC19–DC24.

33 Ansari, A., Munir, K., & Gregg, T. (2012). "Impact at the 'bottom of the pyramid': The role of social capital in capability development and community empowerment." *Journal of Management Studies* 49 (4): 813–42.

34 Bradley, S.W., McMullen, J.S., Artz, K., & Simiyu, E.M. (2012). "Capital is not enough: Innovation in developing economies." *Journal of Management Studies* 49 (4): 684–718.

35 Hall, J., Matos, S., Sheehan, L., & Silvestre, B. (2012). "Entrepreneurship and innovation at the base of the pyramid: A recipe for inclusive growth or social exclusion?" *Journal of Management Studies* 49 (4): 785–812.

36 Lehmann, U., & Sanders, D. (2007). "Community health workers: What do we know about them? The state of the evidence on programmes, activities, costs and impact on health outcomes of using community health workers." *World Health Organization Evidence and Information for Policy.* Geneva: Department of Human Resources for Health. Retrieved 24 January 2013 from: http://www.who.int/hrh/documents/community_health_workers.pdf.

37 Cash, R., Wikler, D., Saxena, A., Capron, A., & Gutnick, R. (Eds). (2009). *Casebook on ethical issues in international health research.* Geneva: World Health Organization. Retrieved 20 November 2012 from: http://whqlibdoc .who.int/publications/2009/9789241547727_eng.pdf.

38 Merton, R.K. (1936). "The unintended consequences of purposive social action." *American Sociological Review* 1 (6): 894–904. Retrieved 24 January 2013 from: http://www.d.umn.edu/cla/faculty/jhamlin/4111/Readings /MertonSocialAction.pdf.

39 McGahan (2012), "Paradoxes of innovation in health and their resolution in embedded innovation."

40 IDRC (2012), Retrieved 20 November 2012 from: http://www.idrc.ca /EN/Programs/Science_and_Innovation/Innovation_for_Inclusive _Development/Pages.

41 Hum, R., Jha, P., McGahan, A., & Cheng, Y.-L. (2012). "Global divergence in critical income for adult and childhood survival 2007: Analyses of mortality using Michaelis-Menten." *eLife* 1:e00051.

42 Klein, P., Mahoney, J., McGahan, M.A., & Pitelis, C. (2011). "Strategy and the Libecap paradox: Efficiency and co-adaptation of organizations and institutions." Working paper (February).

6

Scaling Up: The Case of Nutritional Interventions in the Global South

ASHLEY AIMONE PHILLIPS
NANDITA PERUMAL
CARMEN HO
STANLEY ZLOTKIN

Introduction

Much of the literature on innovation has focused on the Global North. When these models of innovation are applied in low- and middle-income countries, value is typically provided for the "haves" while overlooking – and in some cases excluding – the "have-nots." The challenges specific to the Global South demand a different approach to properly address the needs of the poor. As noted in the introduction to this book, this approach is about adapting existing interventions to particular contexts so as to avoid potentially regressive consequences. It is also rooted in the recognition that what were previously considered "simple fixes" to "simple problems" actually require complex processes at every stage from discovery to implementation. In the case of interventions that have been demonstrated to be successful on a small scale, the next critical step in the process is scaling up to expand coverage and thus reach a greater number of people. However, as McGahan, Rezaie, and Cole note in chapter 5, there is an inherent tension between replication and contextualization that can present significant challenges in the scaling process. This chapter therefore focuses on scaling and how we can successfully overcome the challenges associated with this complex yet critical step in innovating for the Global South.

Our particular area of focus is child undernutrition, which is an underlying cause of one-third of child deaths in sub-Saharan Africa and southern Asia and a persistent global health issue. While efforts to address undernutrition are merited solely on humanitarian grounds, the economic consequences of undernourishment also make it a critical issue to address. Children who survive undernutrition have stunted growth and compromised brain development. Productivity losses from poor physical status and cognitive functioning have been well documented, contributing to reduced earning potential later in life. Decreases in income can bring about consumption deprivation, forced de-accumulation, and traps of pernicious borrowing, locking individuals into a cycle of poverty and undernutrition. The deprivations of undernutrition are therefore inextricably linked to poverty, hindering rapid progress towards the Millennium Development Goals (MDGs).

Several effective nutrition interventions currently exist, and while concerted efforts to promote and scale up these interventions are underway, there is very little consensus on the most effective way to go to scale, with a number of conceptual and operational frameworks involving a myriad of different approaches. In the sections that follow, we describe "scaling up" in the context of nutrition interventions and provide examples of general scaling frameworks from the published literature. We then draw upon the peer-reviewed and grey literature to distil key "lessons learned" from past successes and challenges, highlighting common themes. We conclude that there is a significant need for more effective monitoring and evaluation of scaling processes and outcomes, as well as knowledge translation and communication to ensure that ongoing and future scaling efforts have positive impacts.

Scaling Up Nutrition Interventions

Since the Millennium Development Goals (MDGs) were declared and the first MDG dedicated to eradicating extreme poverty and hunger, an abundance of knowledge has been generated on the subject of child undernutrition and effective solutions to this public health issue. Based on this work, a series in the *Lancet* identified a set of interventions with proven efficacy for improving maternal and child nutrition in 2008.[1] The following year, a study by the World Bank refined the list and prioritized interventions according to estimated programmatic feasibility and cost effectiveness.[2] However, in most countries with high rates of undernutrition, effective interventions are not being scaled up to reach the most undernourished children.[3] In response, reports released by the United Nations and other peer-reviewed publications have called for concentrated efforts and accelerated action in scaling up these nutrition interventions.[4]

The idea of scaling up is to take an intervention that has been successful in one context and expand the relevant policies, programs, or projects so the intervention can benefit more people. This can encompass many dimensions, including scaling up *inputs*, so that more funds or a greater number of staff are mobilized; scaling up *outputs*, so that more services are provided; scaling up *outcomes*, to reach more people and increase client utilization; and scaling up *impact*, to reduce morbidity and mortality. In addition to expanding inputs, outputs, outcomes, and impact, two critical components of scaling involve *adapting* these solutions to their new contexts and *sustaining* their implementation.[5] More specifically, it is important to consider the different environmental contexts and adapt solutions accordingly.[6] Scaling must also be approached with sustainability in mind, and steps need to be taken to ensure the institutionalization of the intervention in policies, program guidelines, and budgets[7] so that the solution can be regularly provided over the needed period of time.

The literature contains a number of conceptual and operational frameworks for scaling up, some of which have been summarized below. What is lacking, however, is consensus on which framework should be adopted or a suggested methodology for choosing or combining frameworks.for a particular scaling context. Whether this has led to inconsistent success in scaling is not clear, and thus we searched the literature for "on-the-ground" examples of scaled up nutritional (micronutrient) interventions targeted to children between birth and five years of age. We compare not only the approaches used but also key success factors and critical challenges for scaling.

Scaling Framework Examples

Theoretical frameworks conceptualizing the processes involved in scaling up began to emerge in the early 1980s. Among these earlier works, Myers[8] contributed a seminal piece on expanding the coverage and impact of health interventions and emphasized the need for a systematized method for achieving scale. Three decades later, several frameworks for taking interventions to scale have enhanced our understanding of scaling processes (see appendix 1). These frameworks aim to define what "scaling up" means and identify the approaches and dimensions involved in scaling. Each framework further explores the dynamics that enable scaling processes; some also attempt to operationalize the steps in taking an innovation to scale. In spite of differences in the approaches for achieving scale, there are common themes that have proven fundamental to our understanding of scaling.

It is generally agreed that having a feasible plan is essential for scale-up success. This plan should address the *what*, *how*, and *who* aspects of the scaling process. In other words, *what* will be scaled up? *How* will scale-up occur? And *who* will champion the scale-up process? In terms of deciding *what* to scale up, whether it is an innovation, process, or program, scale-up should not occur until an intervention has demonstrated efficacy and effectiveness in achieving targeted outcomes and has been simplified so as to be amenable to scaling. The most common examples of what to scale emerge from pilot-phase or demonstration projects that have first demonstrated efficacy on a small scale.

At the same time, the *how* of scaling up has garnered substantial discussion and research to delineate the strategies (or organizational paths) for scaling. There are three broad approaches through which interventions can achieve scale:

i   *Expansion* (also referred to as "horizontal scaling") refers to taking a model to scale by increasing the coverage and size of the implementing organization. This generally means that small, pilot-phase applications are implemented at a larger scale by the same organization. Expansion can also occur through "mainstreaming," where implementing organizations increase impact through training and knowledge generation.
ii *Explosion* (also referred to as "spontaneous diffusion," "vertical scaling," or "political scaling") involves going directly to scale at the country or regional level, often in response to changes in legislation, and thus tends to by-pass the pilot phase. This approach requires innovations to be institutionalized across sectors ("vertical scaling") and involves additional stakeholder groups in the scale-up process so that systems and structures can be adapted and resources redistributed appropriately. Scaling up by *replication* is similar to *explosion* in that it involves increasing the use of an innovation by increasing

the number of adopting organizations (in the public or private sector), a process that ultimately leads to policy change.

iii *Associations* (synonymous with "collaborations") refers to a strategy of scaling up in which programs of similar aims in different regions are linked together to establish an integrated network of collaboration and reach. This approach requires innovative partnerships and governance structures (e.g., *strategic alliances*) in order to organize collaborative efforts for large-scale implementation.

Several frameworks consider the "dimension of scaling," which can be geographic, referring to an extension in coverage to new locations;[9] technological, which refers to an increase in the scope of activities or services provided;[10] political or institutional, which refers to a wider stakeholder participation to influence political processes;[11] economic, which refers to how much it costs to scale up; or temporal, which refers to how long it will take to scale up.[12] These dimensions highlight the multi-sectoral nature of planning the scale-up process.

A related consideration is determining *who* will champion the scaling process. Potential implementing organizations may include non-governmental organizations (NGOs), public sector agencies, private voluntary organizations, consulting firms, or community-based organizations. Not only is it critical to identify an implementing organization, it is also important to define specific roles and responsibilities, ranging from advocacy to transdisciplinary communication. In fact, the capacity of the implementing organization is critically important for long-term sustainability.

Lastly, several scaling frameworks underline the importance of context-specific adaptation – innovations that are feasible in one context are not necessarily relevant or applicable in others – and of monitoring and evaluation, as essential elements in the scaling process. Context-specific adaptation is important for scaling success, as it addresses the political environment, institutional capacity, available inputs and resources, and legal frameworks specific to a country or regional context. There is wide consensus among those responsible for working within frameworks that scaling up is a learning process that requires not only adaptation but also flexibility and openness to change. To this extent, monitoring progress and evaluating impacts can help to facilitate the learning process by identifying challenges and enhancing our understanding of the costs and benefits of scaling up.

Scaling Up Micronutrient (Mineral and Vitamin) Interventions for Children: Examples from the Literature

Scaling Approaches Used

A total of ten papers describing scaled-up micronutrient interventions, either individually or as part of a program, were retrieved from the peer-reviewed and grey literature (see appendix 2). The literature review method is described in appendix 3. With the exception of a program in Madagascar, none of the scaling approaches or strategies appeared to be based on a conceptual or operational framework, and all were planned and carried out deliberately (rather than through spontaneous diffusion). The types of sub-approaches used varied across countries, ranging from horizontal (e.g., replication or expansion) to vertical (e.g., driven by policy or political initiatives) to diversification (e.g., adding a new intervention to an existing program or initiative). The organizational choices or strategies for promoting scale-up of an intervention were primarily additive, since there tended to be one organization responsible for planning and implementing the scale-up effort with the support of a single resource team.

Key Success Factors

Several factors for successful scaling have been reported in the literature, most of which pertain to the structure of the scaling environment, emphasizing the importance of partnerships, multi-sectoral involvement, community participation, and government leadership and policy commitment. Other recurring themes included those relating to the characteristics of the intervention itself, as well as to supply and delivery. Also mentioned is the importance of monitoring and evaluation.

Increasing service delivery, financing, or stewardship typically involves the coordination of several organizations to expand reach.[13] The involvement of several players, ranging from grassroots NGOs to local and federal governments to international organizations and funders, can result in fairly complex coalitions that need to form effective working partnerships. The increasing role of the private sector, which has become more engaged in finding solutions to undernutrition,[14] has led to new public-private partnerships for food fortification. These partnerships include National Fortification Alliances, International Business Alliances, the International Business Leaders Forum hosted at Harvard

University, GAIN Business Alliance, and the Flour Fortification Initiative, and complement the traditional NGO or government programs.

There is also a general recognition that undernutrition has many causes and can only effectively be addressed by engaging different sectors. As such, a key to successful scaling up is effective multi-sectoral involvement. For example, agriculture, health, and social protection all play a role in nutrition levels, and the integration of nutrition programs into different sectors is of great importance. When this is done in a coherent fashion, so that all government policies are coordinated to achieve intended results, literature has described an increase in the effectiveness of scaling.

Government leadership and policy commitment also play a key role. The presence of political will and the support of national policies can greatly facilitate scaling-up initiatives,[15] as scaling up needs leadership, vision, and shared values. Leaders need to drive the roll-out, institutions need a clear set of objectives to navigate the process, and individuals within institutions need appropriate incentives to carry out the scaling. Mutually supportive and carefully coordinated policies, programs, and projects (including laws, regulations, and norms) will therefore facilitate the process. At the same time, the community needs to participate in the scaling process. This involves engaging community members or community health workers in the planning, implementation, and monitoring of interventions.[16]

The characteristics of the intervention are also important. Simple interventions have had greater levels of success,[17] and it is, in fact, recommended that innovations be simplified to their most essential components.[18] The supply and delivery of these interventions is also critical to the process, requiring robust partnerships, multi-sectoral collaborations, and programs and policies that facilitate the delivery of interventions.

Finally, there is a strong consensus that careful and well-designed monitoring and evaluation are crucial to effective scaling.[19] Monitoring is a catalyst not only for maintaining momentum and accountability but for keeping the scaling-up process on track.[20] It helps in assessing progress relative to objectives and identifying aspects that are not working well, and thus allows decision makers to make informed choices.[21] However, monitoring is often neglected, and routine monitoring is rarely used to inform scaling.[22] This undermines interveners' ability to track the effects of the new model and make adjustments if results differ from what is intended. Documentation of the innovation and its impact is therefore essential.[23]

Critical Challenges

While many key success factors have been reported in the literature, there is a noticeable lack of research on "what does not work" in going to scale. First, while success factors can help facilitate the process of scaling, critical challenges may act as important constraints to effective scaling up. Although scaling frameworks provide guidance, there is no consensus on which approaches are optimal or how frameworks can be combined to address specific situations. Without a robust body of evidence to make informed decisions, program planners and policy makers are left with an incomplete picture of *how* these interventions should be implemented, *where* financial support and human resources should be focused, and *who* should be responsible for the scaling process.

Second, there has been limited sharing of "lessons learned" in the scaling process. In our review of micronutrient interventions, only one study notes that "ensuring high (intervention) acceptance and adherence among beneficiaries"[24] is a critical challenge in scaling up micronutrient powders in refugee camps and emergency situations. Other studies provide limited information on the barriers faced in their scale-up efforts, and few document scaling failures.

Furthermore, insight on how to scale up equitably has been limited. This is of particular concern, as inequities in health coverage, disaggregated by age, gender, and geographical area, have been reported in many contexts.[25] Therefore, while the objective may be to roll interventions out quickly, it is important to achieve a balance between speed and equity so as to target the most, "poor and vulnerable groups, which tend to be the hardest to reach."[26] Special attention must to be paid to ensure that solutions are accessible to vulnerable and underserved populations, a particular challenge in resource-constrained settings.

Third, resource constraints in the Global South pose additional challenges. In many low- and middle-income countries, governments lack the financial resources to scale up interventions effectively. At the same time, they may be crippled by health-care systems that are incapable of implementing interventions on a large scale. The problem can be compounded by limitations in human resources, infrastructure and equipment, and medical supplies that, in turn, reduce the countries' ability to take an intervention to scale. While understanding the complexities surrounding scaling up can help identify potential barriers,[27] "studying implementation at the local level"[28] cannot in itself overcome resource constraints and the subsequent barriers to delivery and implementation.

Customized strategies are needed, rather than a "one size fits all" approach, to facilitate country-specific initiatives in scaling up, so that local institutions are involved in meeting challenges in the local contexts.[29] Arguably, implementation science plays an invaluable role in overcoming these constraints. The investigation of research questions that directly address the resource constraints in scaling, such as "how best to train and incentivize ... community health workers" and "how best to engage non-state actors, including NGOs and the private sector, in scale up efforts," have been noted as critically important.[30] Encouraging implementation research is therefore an important strategy for tackling the challenges in taking interventions to scale.

The Importance of Knowledge Translation and Communication

While efforts to scale up interventions have substantially increased in recent years, and there have been documented cases of success, the widespread achievement of MDG 1 ("eradication of extreme poverty and hunger") remains limited. We argue that this is likely because of a gap between the research on "what works" in scaling up and the translation of this research into practice. For instance, recommended actions for achieving MDG 1 are provided without suggested strategies, resources, or support mechanisms for implementing these actions, with the result that the knowledge gained in one case cannot easily be adapted and applied to the local context of countries with a high burden of malnutrition.[31] Furthermore, the rate of progress in scaling up interventions has been considerably slowed because of limited opportunities for sharing experiences and the lessons learned from the successes and failures of others.

It is critical, then, for the global health community to invest substantial effort in bridging the "know-do gap, the gap between what is known and what gets done in practice."[32] Only recently has the need for knowledge translation strategies that effectively communicate and evaluate the progress towards MDG 1 driven the development of more coordinated, systems-based approaches, such as the Scaling Up Nutrition (SUN) "framework for action" and Road Map. The SUN "framework for action" provides a structured means through which governments of high-burden countries can establish and pursue collaborative multi-sectoral efforts to scale up nutrition. Specifically, the SUN framework is an exemplary case for knowledge translation because it identifies the multiple stakeholders critical to scaling nutrition interventions and brings together key actors under one framework to strengthen the individual and collective capacity of experts and policy makers in leading change.[33] The increasing use of approaches that promote collaboration across sectors within countries and the building of efficient communication channels to allow knowledge to be translated across national and international borders may signify the beginning of a paradigm shift from the confines of vertical programming to a systems perspective.

However, evaluating the success of the SUN framework will rely heavily on rigorous monitoring and evaluation. Collecting data to quantify scaling-up efforts and consistently using these data in evaluating progress towards program targets are essential and often overlooked aspects of scaling-up and knowledge-sharing practice. Effective use of monitoring and evaluation strategies can provide critical information regarding improvements in indicators for health system strengthening and equitable coverage. Emphasizing the value in collecting monitoring data, analysing these data, and packaging the information so it can be easily used by decision makers are critical for making progress in scaling-up efforts. Effectively communicating the knowledge gained and lessons learned can decrease inefficiencies in scaling up and foster a shared responsibility in decreasing undernutrition.[34] In sum, coordinated efforts for the sharing of knowledge have the potential to bring about the widespread implementation of evidence-based, cost-effective interventions that improve overall health and well-being in all corners of the world.

Conclusions

This chapter draws upon frameworks from the peer-reviewed literature to identify key success factors and critical challenges in scaling up health interventions. We found that partnerships, multi-sectoral involvement, community participation, government leadership, and policy commitment are commonly agreed to be important considerations for taking interventions to scale. Other recurring themes pertain to the characteristics of the intervention itself, as well as to supply and delivery issues and monitoring and evaluation. Yet several effective interventions for alleviating micronutrient malnutrition have only reached scale in specific country contexts. This finding underscores the challenges of scaling up, including a lack of consensus in frameworks, financial and human resource constraints, and limitations in research into ways of overcoming implementation barriers in scaling up. Emphasis on monitoring progress, evaluating data, and developing effective communication strategies to translate knowledge into practice is therefore critically important.

Acknowledgments

The authors would like to thank the instructors of the International Health Systems course (HAD5768) in the Department of Health Policy Management and Evaluation, University of Toronto, for their contributions to the conception of this review and critical appraisal of previous work related to the manuscript.

THE IDEA IN BRIEF

"Scaling up" refers to the process of taking an intervention that has been successful in one context and expanding the relevant policies, programs, or projects so that the intervention can benefit more people. There is, however, an inherent tension between replication and contextualization, making scaling up a complex process. In fact, there is little consensus on how to effectively go to scale, with a number of frameworks citing different approaches. It is therefore critical to review past cases of scaling, so as to identify key factors for success and critical challenges to overcome.

IMPLICATIONS

1 As successful interventions need to be scaled up in order to effectively progress towards the achievement of the Millennium Development Goals, greater attention needs to be paid to documenting scaling up experiences and better understanding what works and what does not work
2 Knowledge-mobilization strategies that effectively translate research into action can be very useful for successfully going to scale

FOOD FOR THOUGHT

How can international organizations, national and local governments, and civil society organizations improve their ability to share knowledge and translate research into action to scale up interventions? And how can a generalized framework for scaling be adapted to better address context-specific demands?

Appendices

Appendix 1:
Ten Scaling Frameworks Identified from the Literature Search

1 Bezanson, K., & Isenman, P. (2010). "Scaling up nutrition: A framework for action." Policy Brief. *Food and Nutrition Bulletin* 31 (1): 178–86.
2 Bhandari, N., Kabir, A.K., & Salam, M.A. (2008). "Mainstreaming nutrition into maternal and child health programmes: Scaling up of exclusive breastfeeding." *Maternal and Child Nutrition* 4 (Suppl. 1) (April): 5–23. ISSN 1740–8709.
3 Bryce, J., Victora, C.G., Boerma, T., Peters, D.H., & Black, R.E. (2011). "Evaluating the scale-up for maternal and child survival: A common framework." *International Health* 3: 139–46.
4 Cooley, L., & Kohl, R. (2006). *Scaling up - From vision to large scale change: A management framework for practitioners.* Washington, DC: Management Systems International (MSI).
5 Gonsalves, J. (2000). "Going to scale: Can we bring more benefits to more people more quickly?" Workshop highlights presented by CGIAR-NGO Committee and Global Forum for Agricultural Research. (10–14 April). Silang, Cavite, Philippines: International Institute of Rural Reconstruction.
6 Hartmann, A., & Linn, J. (2008). *Scaling up: A framework and lessons for development effectiveness from literature and practice.* Washington, DC: Brookings Institution.
7 Myers, R. (1984). "Going to scale." UNICEF Meeting on Community Based Child Development. New York: Consultative Group on Early Childhood Care and Development.
8 Simmons, R., Fajans, P., & Ghiron, L. (2007). *Scaling up health service delivery: From pilot innovations to policies and programmes.* Geneva: World Health Organization.
9 Uvin, P., Jain, P.S., & Brown, L.D. (2000). "Think large and act small: Towards a new paradigm for NGO scaling up." *World Development* 28: 1409–19.
10 Yamey, G. (2011). "Scaling up global health interventions: A proposed framework for success." *Public Library of Science Medicine* 8 (6) (June): e1001049. ISSN 1549–1676.

Appendix 2:
Ten Papers Describing Scaled-Up Nutrition Interventions for Children (0 to 5 Years) in Low- and Middle-Income Countries Retrieved from the Peer-Reviewed and Grey Literature

1 Haselow, N.J. (2004). "Reaching the end of the road in Africa: Using community-directed treatment with ivermectin to deliver vitamin A supplements." Helen Keller International.
2 American Red Cross. (2004). "Partnerships in action: An integrated approach to combining a measles campaign with a bed net, vitamin A and mebendazole campaign in Zambia."
3 Melgarejo, C.H., & Mildon, A. (2005). "Effectiveness of home-based fortification of complementary foods with Sprinkles in an integrated nutrition program to address rickets and anemia." Ulaanbaatar: World Vision Mongolia.
4 Lechtig, A., Gross, R., Vivanco, O.A., Gross, U., & López de Romaña, D. (2006). "Lessons learned from the scaling-up of a weekly multimicronutrient supplementation program in the integrated food security program (PISA)." *Food and Nutrition Bulletin* 27 (4) (Suppl. Peru): S160–5.
5 Sanghvi, T., Dary, O., & Houston, R. (2007). "Part 3: How can vitamin and mineral deficiencies be reduced? Implementing proven interventions at scale." *Food and Nutrition Bulletin* 28 (1): S182–96.
6 Larson, C.P., Roy, S.K., Khan, A.I., Rahman, A.S., & Qadri, F. (2008). "Zinc treatment to under-five children: Applications to improve child survival and reduce burden of disease." *Health and Population Nutrition* 26 (3): 356–65.
7 Guyon, A.B., Quinn, V.J., Hainsworth, M., Ravonimanantsoa, P., Ravelojoana, V., Rambeloson, Z., & Martin, L. (2009). "Implementing an integrated nutrition package at large scale in Madagascar: The Essential Nutrition Actions framework." *Food and Nutrition Bulletin* 30 (3): 233–44.
8 Kalimbira, A.A., MacDonald, C., & Simpson, J.R. (2010). "The impact of an integrated community-based micronutrient and health programme on stunting in Malawian preschool children." *Public Health Nutrition* 13 (5): 720–9.
9 Wuehler, S.E., & Ly Wane, C.T. (2011). "Situational analysis of infant and young child nutrition policies and programmatic activities in Senegal." *Maternal and Child Nutrition* 7 (Suppl 1): 157–81.
10 Rah, J.H., dePee, S., Kraemer, K., Steiger, G., Bloem, M.W., Spiegel, P., et al. (2012). "Program experience with micronutrient powders and current evidence." *Journal of Nutrition* 142 (1): 191S–196S.

Appendix 3
Literature Review Methods

Potential papers were identified in the peer-reviewed and grey literature by searching journal databases (Pubmed, Medline, Embase, Scopus, Web of Science), United Nations (UN) agency and non-governmental organization (NGO) websites, the University of Toronto library catalogue, and Google Scholar. Hand searches of the reference sections of selected sources were conducted to identify additional scaling-related material. These sources included working groups and not-for-profit organizations such as ExpandNet (www.expandnet.net), the CORE Group (www.coregroup.org), and MEASURE Evaluation (www.cpc.unc.edu). Search terms and relevance criteria were adjusted in order to identify examples of scaled-up nutrition interventions for young children (less than five years of age) living in low- and middle-income countries. Qualitative data synthesis was used to compare selected papers in terms of the types of scaling approaches used, reported factors of success or challenges, as well as the actual or potential impact of the scaled-up interventions at national and international levels (where applicable). The efficiency of knowledge translation strategies for communicating and evaluating progress was assessed by comparing the MDG and "Scaling Up Nutrition" (SUN) progress reports in terms of how undernutrition was measured and reported; how progress targets were set, addressed, and evaluated; how knowledge was translated; and how process improvements were determined and supported.

REFERENCES

1 Bryce, J., Coitinho, D., Darnton-Hill, I., Pelletier, D., & Pinstrup-Andersen, P. (2008). "Maternal and child undernutrition: Effective action at national level." *Lancet* 371 (9611): 510–26.
2 Horton, S., Shekar, M., McDonald, C., Mahal, A., & Brooks, J.K. (2009). *Scaling up nutrition: What will it cost?* Washington, DC: World Bank.
3 Bryce et al. (2008), "Maternal and child undernutrition."
4 United Nations. (2011). *The Millennium Development Goals Report.* New York: United Nations.
5 Hartmann, A., & Linn, J. (2008). *Scaling up: A framework and lessons for development effectiveness from literature and practice.* Washington, DC: Brookings Institution.
6 WHO/ExpandNet. Retrieved March 2012 from: www.expandnet..net.
7 Ibid.

8   Myers, R. (1984). "Going to scale." UNICEF Meeting on Community Based
    Child Development. New York: Consultative Group on Early Childhood
    Care and Development.
9   Hartmann & Linn (2008), "Scaling up."
10 Gonsalves, J. (2000). "Going to scale: Can we bring more benefits to more
    people more quickly?" Silang, Cavite, Philippines: International Institute
    of Rural Reconstruction.
11 Ibid.
12 Hartmann & Linn (2008), "Scaling up"; and Gonsalves (2000), "Going to
    scale."
13 Simmons, R., Fajans, P., & Ghiron, L. (2007). *Scaling up health service deliv-*
    ery: From pilot innovations to policies and programmes. Geneva: World Health
    Organization.
14 Scaling Up Nutrition (SUN) Road Map Task Team. (2010). *A road map for scal-*
    ing up nutrition. 159. Retrieved March 2012 from: www.scalingupnutrition.org.
15 Yamey, G. (2011). "Scaling up global health interventions: A proposed
    framework for success." *Public Libraries of Science Medicine* 8 (6): e1001049.
16 Ibid.
17 Ibid.
18 WHO/ExpandNet.
19 Hartmann & Linn (2008), "Scaling up."
20 Cooley, L., & Kohl, R. (2006). *Scaling up - From vision to large scale change:*
    A management framework for practitioners. Washington, DC: Management
    Systems International (MSI).
21 Simmons, Fajans, & Ghiron, (2007), *Scaling up health service delivery.*
22 Ibid.
23 WHO/ExpandNet.
24 Rah, J.H., dePee, S., Kraemer, K., Steiger, G., Bloem, M.W., Spiegel, P., et
    al. (2010). "Program experience with micronutrient powders and current
    evidence." *Journal of Nutrition* 142 (1): 191S–196S.
25 Welch, V., Ueffing, E., & Tugwell, P. (2009). "Knowledge translation: An
    opportunity to reduce global health inequalities," *Journal of International*
    Development 21 (November).
26 Mangham, L., & Hanson, K. (2010). "Scaling up in international health:
    What are the key issues?" *Health Policy and Planning* 25.
27 Ibid.
28 Yamey (2011), "Scaling up global health interventions."
29 Subramanian, S., Naimoli, J., Matsubayashi, T., & Peters, D.H. (2011). "Do
    we have the right models for scaling up health services to achieve the Mil-
    lennium Development Goals?" *BMC Health Services Research* 11 (336).

30 Yamey (2011), "Scaling up global health interventions."
31 G-20 Multi-Year Action Plan. (2011). "Scaling up knowledge sharing for development." A working paper for the G-20 Development Working Group, Pillar 9.
32 Pablos-Mendez, A., & Shademai, R. (2006). "Knowledge translation in global health." *Journal of Continuing Education in the Health Professions* 26 (160).
33 G-20 Multi-Year Action Plan (2011), "Scaling up knowledge sharing for development."
34 Ibid. 007

7

New Models for Financing Innovative Technologies and Entrepreneurial Organizations in the Global South

MURRAY R. METCALFE

We are continually faced with a series of great opportunities brilliantly disguised as insoluble problems.

– John Gardner (1912–2002), Citizen Sector pioneer

But I am an impatient optimist. The world is getting better, but it's not getting better fast enough, and it's not getting better for everyone.

– Bill Gates (at the World Economic Forum, Davos, Switzerland, January 2008)

Introduction

The development of the Global South in the twenty-first century will look nothing like what twentieth-century models based on foreign aid and multilateral agencies envisioned. Instead, real development will stem from two familiar forces – technology innovation and local, entrepreneurship-focused new enterprises (not necessarily in that order). The present trickle of financial support for these new approaches will rapidly expand as the twentieth-century models of aid are abandoned and replaced by financing approaches that more closely resemble those that have supported the technology/entrepreneur nexus in the Global North. What will the new set of financing organizations and mechanisms look like, and what will propel them forward? What are the cutting-edge examples of this trend? Will twentieth-century models be dismantled rapidly, given their deep entrenchment in huge bureaucracies?

The powerful linkage of technology innovation and entrepreneurship is seen in the twentieth-century development in the Global North of massive industries, including semiconductors, computing, software, the Internet, and biotechnology. The models often stem from Silicon Valley and the United States. In Taiwan and selected other Asian countries that have emerged as world leaders in the second half of the twentieth century, these models have helped lift the standard of living in the country by orders of magnitude.

But as one turns to the development of the most impoverished nations, these technology/entrepreneurship models are in short supply, and the twentieth-century history of foreign aid has been based on a totally different model. More recently, scholars and practitioners, led by William Easterly, formerly of the World Bank and now of New York University,[1] have questioned the effectiveness of these aid-driven models. Easterly differentiates the existing dominant model, one led by a limited and elite cadre of Northern "planners," from the alternative "on the ground" models based on the collective efforts of many more "searchers" – or, as many of us would call these individuals and organizations, entrepreneurs. As Easterly says, "the right plan is to have no plan" – a statement that confuses students, as they take it to mean that small organizations should not plan. What Easterly is focusing on is planning on a small scale as compared to the sprawling, top-down plans of the multilateral-development financing bodies. Easterly contrasts the lack of success of the aid-based models, in the case, say, of distributing inexpensive doses of malaria vaccines, with the logistical mechanisms that allow the global deployment of millions of copies of new Harry Potter books overnight.

The success of the Northern technology/entrepreneur innovation model has depended heavily on financing techniques driven not by government grants and subsidies but by risk capital approaches such as venture capital (VC) and its variants. Experiments have begun that adapt those financing models for use in the developing world. The features are the same as in the North – backing entrepreneurs/searchers who are working on the ground with deep local knowledge and who are inventing and/or adopting innovative business models, some of which are driven by or strongly enabled by information technology and other advances. In some cases, the technology developed is itself unique and highly innovative; in other (often equally effective) cases, the technology has been previously deployed and is better understood. These financing techniques promise possible upside rewards but carry risk with them. There may be more failures than successes. In the long term, the successes more than compensate for the failures, but that approach only works with careful due diligence and scrutiny by the investor group. "We take risks by being very careful" is how one U.S.-based venture capital investor recently expressed it to this observer.

This chapter examines the components of these new financing models in the context of development, the components of the innovation system, and how those elements are combined, and also speculates (in advance of a more thorough treatment in chapter 8) on the implications for the old models of aid and more broadly for sustainable development.

Entrepreneurial Organizations

We are all familiar with models of the combined power of entrepreneurship and technology, sometimes with innovative financing approaches. Early-twentieth-century examples include Laurence S. Rockefeller and family's backing of the creation of Eastern Airlines (originally LSR Eastern Airlines) and McDonnell Aircraft Corporation, and ultimately the commercial aviation sector as we know it today. But it is the rise of Silicon Valley beginning in the 1970s that still reverberates today, starting with the founding of Fairchild Semiconductor (by, among others, Eugene Kleiner, later a founder of Kleiner, Perkins, Caulfield and Byers, still a leading Silicon Valley VC firm) and then Intel Corporation (funded initially by legendary VC pioneer Arthur Rock and later Venrock, a Rockefeller family investment arm). The examples continue in terms of additional current-day pillars of the technology world – Apple, Microsoft, Google, Facebook. And this movement eventually branched into totally different segments, notably including the life sciences segment and the founding of Genentech by Robert Swanson and Herbert Boyer, an initiative that represented the birth of the global biotechnology industry.

These enterprise models were not confined to the United States. Sony, founded by Akio Morita and Masura Ibuka, came from what was then a developing country – Japan – and in fact helped lead that country out of its post-Second World War economic depression. Although the technology was American – transistors – the idea of using that technology in low-priced consumer-oriented products like pocket radios was revolutionary. This model of creative replication and application of existing technologies is well documented in the case of Taiwan.

The model has since continued in the Global South, albeit with more limited examples. The Mittal family, an Indian family of modest origins, founded what is today Arcelor Mittal, the largest steel producer in the world. Other Indian success stories include Infosys and other major firms in the outsourcing segment, and Suzlon in wind turbines. The story of Tulsi Tanti and Suzlon is particularly impressive in that it involves technology components that are difficult to construct and transport. The Tanti family started as small textile yarn manufacturers – and built Suzlon through business model insights regarding the needs of similar customers in the context of an unreliable electricity grid in India. They used available commercial financing approaches to further build Suzlon through the strategic acquisition of financially troubled European component and systems providers. In the African cell phone segment, Mohamed "Mo" Ibrahim built a giant service provider, Celtel, with the assistance of American and British financial backers.

Social entrepreneurs are similar in productivity to commercial entrepreneurs but build enterprises with social goals rather than primarily commercial/economic goals. Well-documented and -recognized examples include Grameen Bank, BRAC, and the Aravind Eye Hospital (as described in chapter 1). These organizations began with limited resources and generally were not highly dependent on initial financing from government or international funding bodies.

Efforts to assist the social entrepreneurship movement in global development in the South have centred on empowering entrepreneurs through knowledge, support, and (often limited) capital. A group of organizations based in the North has emerged over time to support social entrepreneurs in the South, notably Ashoka, founded in 1981 by the American Bill Drayton. The core of the Ashoka model is a revolving group of Ashoka Fellows, who can be based anywhere in the world. Ashoka provides, for a limited number of years, a salary and a support grant, and, importantly, links to a global community of fellow social entrepreneurs and centralized expertise. In David Bronstein's *How to Change the World*,[2] a series of case studies of early Ashoka Fellows, the case of Fábio Rosa and his work on rural electrification in Brazil vividly demonstrates the isolation of social entrepreneurs and the benefits that may accrue to them in belonging to an extended network of similar socially oriented entrepreneurs. Rosa faced every imaginable hurdle and then some, but persevered and overcame each successive challenge.

In a separate vein from the entrepreneurial model, be it the for-profit Silicon Valley model or social entrepreneurs, the base of pyramid (BOP) literature by Prahalad and Hart [3] and others discusses framing the needs of the poor in the Global South as a market opportunity. Although focused on the role of multinational corporations (MNCs), the Prahalad BOP concept applies equally well to the pursuits of local, profit-driven, small- and medium-scale entrepreneurs and to social entrepreneurs. While critics question the emphasis on marketing – and raise the topic of the marketing of goods that may be not only non-essential but in fact totally discretionary and cosmetic – in reality, today many organizations are offering the most critical necessities to the BOP markets, as discussed below. Prahalad's emphasis on the role of multinational corporations is overdone, although there is no doubt they will play an important role in development of the Global South – which remains a tantalizing market opportunity.[4] But entrepreneurial organizations will also be essential in BOP markets; and they possess a unique ability to assess the needs and consumption patterns of the poor.

Prahalad strongly asserts that new business models will be essential: "To create products and services the poor can afford, MNCs must reduce their costs significantly – to, say, 10 per cent of what they are today. But this cannot be achieved by fine-tuning the current approaches to product development, production, and logistics. The entire business process must be rethought."[5] Of equal importance will be new technologies. Prahalad refutes the notion that only the most sophisticated markets will pay for and use new technologies and that less advanced economies can make do with an older generation of technologies. And Prahalad is eloquent about how these business models and technology innovations will combine to lead to environmentally sustainable development: "among the many possibilities for innovation, MNCs can be leaders in leapfrogging to products that don't repeat the environmental mistakes of developed countries over the last 50 years."[6]

Developing enterprises that are driven by technology, employ innovative business models, and are financed through venture and risk capital is a well-developed art and science. Business and engineering schools around the world teach courses and stage business-plan competitions. Can this model be harnessed in development? The single most critical component of the model is the entrepreneur who understands the technology but can look at markets and, even more, who has a real interest in the customer experience and how unmet customer needs might be met – or, in extreme cases, how new products and services can meet needs that have not even been envisioned.

These entrepreneurs are rare birds – but the supply of talented and motivated candidates in the South is vast. Finding and training them will be a key priority. Calestous Juma and Lee Yee-Cheong cite the examples of the EARTH University in Costa Rica and VIST, set near Lake Victoria in Kenya.[7] Those institutions teach students not to find jobs but rather to be entrepreneurs and employers. The concept extends not just to business school students but to future engineers, lawyers, and government leaders. Can we move those students out of thinking of training in preparation solely for jobs in large corporations and government bodies? This is probably a worthy goal in the North as well, but is of particular importance in the Global South, with massive potential impact.

Technology and Development

In multiple areas we are beginning to see that the limits in solving problems are often not technical; in fact, from a strictly technical perspective, overall solutions to some major issues may be at hand. For example, Mark Jacobson of Stanford is an atmospheric engineer who builds elaborate models of the atmosphere and pollutants. He has done groundbreaking work in comparing, across a broad set of measures, different energy technologies – electricity generation and end-use devices.[8] His work shows that 400,000 to 600,000 wind turbines – large, current-generation 5 MW turbines, appropriately sited – could displace current energy production from all sources in the United States and eliminate 100 per cent of greenhouse gas emissions. Jacobson notes that this does not represent a huge number of turbines when one makes comparisons to, say, aircraft production levels. His models confirm that, because of the conservation of matter, the wind is always blowing somewhere, and intermittency problems can be reduced. So technically our energy problems in North America can be 100 per cent solved using a technology dating to the twelfth century. And of even greater potential, as Ted Sargent of the University of Toronto has noted, "each day the sun bombards us with ten thousand times more energy than we consume."[9]

So, technology can be harnessed to address a broad array of issues in the Global South. But solving these problems is not going to be addressed by technology alone – raising the question of what the other components of innovation systems are. As tempting as it is to trust that advanced technologies will ultimately provide solutions to global challenges, unfortunately it will not be that easy.

The interplay of technology development and organizational structures in a development context can be traced to the pioneering work of Everett Rogers in *Diffusion of Innovations*.[10] The early work of Rogers on the diffusion of innovation centred on hybrid corn seed in Iowa, but he quickly expanded the analysis to topics such as the boiling of drinking water in Peruvian villages. In the latter case, an array of social and cultural barriers prevented the adoption of a demonstrated health innovation. In other cases that Rogers describes, the problem is organizational: for example, it took 150 years from the discovery of how to prevent scurvy on British naval ships to the widespread adoption of the simple solution to the problem. Rogers asks a question that continues to underlie a central enigma of development – why do some things that seem indisputably good ideas propagate rapidly while others fail to catch on and scale? Rogers identifies multiple cultural and environmental factors that combine to determine the outcome in a given setting. His "S-curve" model and key terms such as "early adopter" remain in mainstream use today across a range of fields.

Juma's and Yee-Cheong's tract on technology in support of the Millennium Development Goals describes how three key underlying enablers – infrastructure (of both the bricks and mortar and the communications and computing flavour), higher education (particularly technical education), and a strong cohort of small and medium-size enterprises – surround and pace the deployment of key platform technologies.[11] Those platform technologies – computing and communications, life sciences technologies, nanotechnology, and environmental technology – are the same list as those that would appear as the key investment segments for venture capital firms in the Global North.

Thomas Friedman's *The World Is Flat*[12] is much more contemporary than the work of Rogers but in some ways examines the same question: Why did an enabling technology – low-cost computing and telecommunications – spark an industrial and economic revolution in India but not elsewhere in the developing world? What are the barriers to the further spread of these technologies?

In chapter 3 of this book, Yu-Ling Cheng and Beverly Bradley discuss the role of appropriate technology in development. In chapter 8, Janice Stein makes a strong case for smarter and simpler innovation (i.e., frugal innovation). Our particular goal in this chapter is to discuss how these notions of technology fit within entrepreneurial constructs and risk-financing approaches.

Within these models, a range of technologies, in terms of level of so-phistication, will exist. As described in chapter 3, Paul Polak and others have written on deploying appropriate technologies in the developing world – "design for the other 90%."[13] But perhaps one must question the term "appropriate" – if it is appropriate for them why not for us in the North, and, more pointedly, vice versa? This notion ties again to Prahalad's work on the BOP – we cannot assume that only the North will want and deploy the best technologies. In fact, the notions of Friedman and the flattened world and Easterly's example of the deployment of Western medicines suggest a model of the more universal adoption of advanced technologies such as vaccines, cell phones, and software tools.

Financing Engines

The powerful interaction of technology and entrepreneurial models has been financed in the United States and other centres in the Global North through the rise of the venture capital industry and the related private equity investment segment. In the simplest form, venture capital firms raise a fund of capital from institutions and individuals that they invest in a portfolio of (often, say, twenty) technology ventures. This type of investing is often referred to broadly as risk capital, because of the probability that many of the ventures will fail, a risk that is, however, offset by the possibility of "home runs" elsewhere in the portfolio. The global VC industry today is diverse, but the underlying approach re-mains consistent.

Pioneering Approaches

Efforts have begun to use these risk capital investment models in social settings – in the area that has recently been referred to broadly as im-pact investing – and specifically in the case of investing in enterprises in the developing world serving BOP customers. At the same time, as outlined by Prahalad, the BOP markets are potentially ripe for commer-cial VC and private equity investment. In the former case, those who control pools of philanthropic capital – with the capital often derived from success in Silicon Valley and the technology/entrepreneurship sphere – are coming to believe that impact investing can have a much greater impact on a dollar-for-dollar basis than traditional philanthropy. When Pierre Omidyar and his wife, Pam, achieved liquidity from their roles as the founders of eBay, they initially launched the Omidyar Foundation as a traditional philanthropic entity. But as they realized the restrictions and limits of that model, they converted their foundation to the Omidyar Network, with much greater flexibility as an investment vehicle. Vinod Khosla, another young pillar of the modern Silicon Valley, initially planned to return to India and fund charitable activities – until he realized that he could have much greater impact doing what he had been doing as a VC investor and started Khosla Ventures, a commercial entity.

In the area of global development, multiple organizations, such as Ashoka, fund social entrepreneurs by providing salaries and support grants to enable them to operate. Echoing Green, based in New York, runs a similar program, with the applicant pool increasingly from the Global South.

Perhaps the most pure-play VC model in development is the Acumen Fund, led by Jacqueline Novogratz. New York-based Acumen operates in India, Pakistan, and selected regions of Africa, and has deployed about $70 million of philanthropic capital through a VC model to more than sixty enterprises. The model looks like a conventional commercial VC team. Acumen is organized into matrixed investment teams focused by region and by industry segment. Expertise is shared across the teams, and investment theses and themes emerge over time.

Some of the companies that Acumen has backed are achieving real scale: A to Z Textile Mills (bed nets) in Tanzania; 1298 Ambulance in India; Ecotact, which is a provider of centralized toilet facilities in Kenya; and d.light Design (solar lanterns), a global operation with headquarters in India, customers there and in Africa, manufacturing in China, and a research base in Silicon Valley.

D.light serves as a good example of the power of the model. Founded as a student project at Stanford, d.light marries Silicon Valley expertise with low-cost manufacturing in China. This is then supplemented by a multi-tier distribution network in India and Africa. Engineering is in Silicon Valley, where world-class optical technologies are developed. D.light has been funded not only through Acumen but also by commercial VC sources and by multilateral bodies, notably the IFC (International Finance Corporation) arm of the World Bank.

Certain other Acumen portfolio companies have made use of technologies developed in the North. A to Z Textiles manufactures bed nets using insecticide-embedded materials under licence from Sumitomo of Japan. And 1298 Ambulance uses a familiar technology – Google Maps – to dispatch its crews. But some companies use technologies and, more broadly, business models from the Global South. Husk Power provides village-level electrification in rural Bihar, India, using biomass gasifiers – a technology largely ignored in many parts of the world and perfected in India.

In addition to its activities in health care, energy, housing, and water and sanitation, Acumen has additionally focused more recently on the agricultural segment – a massive part of the BOP economy – and on education. To cite just one example, Acumen has recently invested in BASIX Krishi, in partnership with the BASIX Group, led by Vijay Mahajan. BASIX Krishi provides agricultural extension services to rural farmers for a low annual fee. A network of "Livelihood Service Providers" serves as the local contact point with the customer.

Emergence of More Specialized Models

As in the case of the commercial private equity sector globally, we see that the model has evolved rapidly to include more specialized approaches and related services. "Cleantech" – investing in renewable energy technologies and related environmentally focused products – was a major area of commercial VC activity in the last five years. On the social sector side, a similar concept to Acumen was employed for many years by E + Co., working specifically in the renewable energy sector globally. E + Co. invested across a spectrum of countries and a range of renewable energy technologies, again with the goal of backing sustainable enterprises with the potential to scale.

In terms of other emerging specialized approaches, Imprint Capital in San Francisco has served as an adviser to leading foundations and ultra-high net worth individuals in recommending socially oriented organizations and funds for investment. There have been efforts to build "funds of funds" to invest in a pool of these entities. Chapter 8 describes the Obviam family of funds, a former development arm of the Swiss government, as one example of this movement. ICF has invested $3 billion in capital to date in 190 funds. And finally there is early experimentation with extending the new idea of social impact bonds to development projects. In a social impact bond, a private or institutional investor invests in a program run by an NGO to fund a specific social project. The issuer of the bond (say, a government organization) pays the investor a rate of return on invested capital – but if and only if certain agreed-upon benefits are achieved.[14]

Limits of the Model: Metrics

We know, however, that there are limits to the VC model. The success of the model in the North may have depended on the unique nature of the industries targeted – very high gross margins (i.e., profit margins versus the cost of goods) and goods that could be transported easily and in many cases instantaneously via the Internet and telecom networks. As the models have been applied more broadly, barriers have arisen. The global life sciences sector may be driven by VC money, but given the expense of developing a drug and taking it through the approval process, it is heavily dependent on later-stage corporate support from "big pharma" and other corporate investors, depressing the leverage and returns of earlier stage VC investors. The cleantech sector has yet to take off because of the scale required and the slow pace of change in the energy sector. Vaclav Smil, the Canadian energy economist/historian, has noted that the pace of change in the energy segment can be measured in centuries not years and that the sector has historically relied on government intervention to promote change.[15]

In investing for development and, more generally, in social impact investing, work on metrics continues to evolve. All approaches are a form of "double bottom line" (measuring both economic and social returns) or "triple bottom line" (measuring economics, social impact, and environmental benefits) frameworks. The blended value concept developed by Jed Emerson and others is a further variant. The Acumen Fund has played a leadership role in developing appropriate measures of returns. With the assistance of Google, Acumen developed the PULSE metric system, which has been adopted by a number of other social investment entities. Of course, the difficulty in all cases is determining appropriate and agreed-upon measures of social and environmental impact and then combining the variables in a way that allows the results of a given investment program to be deemed superior to those of another. In a commercial private equity investment, the internal rate of return (IRR) and the multiple of capital returned are commonly used; no such standard shorthand approach exists at present for social- and impact-related investments.

Finally, the failure of many enterprises within a given VC portfolio may raise difficult issues when investments serve the most impoverished and most vulnerable members of society; for example, can the failure of a primary education venture be merely "written off" when there is presumably no opportunity to reconstruct the lost years of learning for young students.

Hybrid Value Chains and Leveraging Entrepreneurial Capital

In addition to the contributions of technology and entrepreneurship, innovation in the developing world will be driven by innovative business models for enterprises and the use of those business models in combination to leverage other major actors in the development sphere.

A thorough depiction of the range of innovation in business model development appears in a review of innovative models in the health-care segment by some of our University of Toronto colleagues.[16] Working from a broader list of organizations from the Global South that they had screened as part of their study, they identified ten health-care organizations and looked at key "business system" elements, including marketing, pricing, operations, and systems. They found that these organizations often innovate in multiple areas simultaneously, leading to unique business models such as the Aravind Eye Care System and 1298 Ambulance, both referred to above. They also found that these organizations have chosen to maintain a focus and resist the temptation to continually broaden and expand. Their success most often derives from business model innovation rather than medical breakthroughs (or technology breakthroughs, in terms of the framework described here).

One current school of thought and experimentation looks at how social enterprises can work within larger networks. The network components include using government funding (such as in the case of 1298 Ambulance) and partnering with progressive multinationals (A to Z Textile Mills). There is also an important role for forward-thinking philanthropic bodies. Acumen was seeded by the Rockefeller Foundation, and has capital from, among others, the Skoll Foundation, the Bill and Melinda Gates Foundation, and one of the philanthropic arms of Google. It is perhaps not a coincidence that the sources of capital in the latter cases stem from some of the greatest success stories in the technology/entrepreneurship sector.

A pioneering approach is building "hybrid value chains." Leaders in developing those concepts include Ashoka's founder and CEO, Bill Drayton, and his colleague Valerie Budinrich,[17] Harvard Business School professor Michael Porter and his colleague Mark Kramer, and Olivier Kayser at Hystra. Hystra is a Paris-based not-for-profit organization that consults to leading corporations that are interested – for multiple reasons – in BOP markets. Hystra's report on the energy sector[18] describes multiple examples of hybrid value chains in that segment. The Hystra energy report assesses each enterprise in terms of its longer-term profitability/sustainability, its effectiveness in delivering on its mission and solving the problem it is addressing, and its likely ability to scale. The framework allows the comparison of a range of different approaches and technologies.

To elaborate on the concept, a "value chain," conceptualized as located within a single enterprise (say, a multinational corporation [MNC]), refers to the series of processes and internal organizations that start with market intelligence and product conceptualization and progress through engineering, production, marketing and pricing, distribution, and delivery to the end customer. A "hybrid value chain" refers to the cases where those steps take place across enterprises and organizations, and specifically involve a not-for-profit organization, or what Drayton and Budinich refer to as a citizen-sector organization (CSO), as a participant. They cite an example of how Ashoka facilitated a partnership of Colcerámica, a subsidiary of a large building-materials retailer in South America, and Kairos, a CSO focused on working with individuals dislocated by armed conflict. "Colcerámica provided the product … and the technical and business know-how (sales and marketing techniques, for instance). Kairos, in return for fees, recruited and managed a female sales force. That model generated income for previously unemployed women and pushed the product into the hands of potential customers, rather than waiting for a storefront to pull them in."[19]

Putting together the key elements of technology, entrepreneurial organizations, risk capital sources, and the additional elements of business models and hybrid value chains yields a depiction of a progressive framework for innovation in the Global South (see figure 7.1). In addition to technology, some of the innovation will be driven by the creative use of ICT (information and communications technologies) and other information systems innovations. Energy, environmental, and sustainability considerations will be paramount, as described below. Once thought of as the domain of civil engineers, the energy footprint and sustainability aspects of products and services are now integral to the engineering design process. In all cases the resulting structure will be adapted to the site and the specific context, and the creativity demonstrated in that process will determine the difference between success and failure in many specific settings. Finally, following from the Everett

Figure 7.1: The Multiple Elements of Innovation in Development

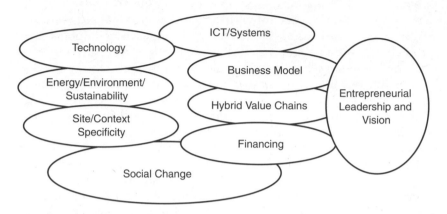

Rogers model, the social change involved will be a key component of the innovation's success.

Aggregating these components in creative ways may represent the future of development. The examples to date are exciting. Another example that perhaps exemplifies the approach is Kiva.org. Kiva is a well-known example that melds the powerful concept of microfinance with online systems as powered by PayPal (a subsidiary of eBay). Kiva allows individuals in the North to serve as microfinance lenders to entrepreneurs (including those in the Global South), in increments as small as $25. On repayment of the loan – and, of course, there are defaults – the lender may choose to recycle the capital into a loan to another entrepreneur. It is not obvious to lenders that their capital is bundled into a broad pool that is in fact channelled through a series of local intermediaries, but the concept is nonetheless strong and the aggregate impact potentially powerful.

The role of governments and multilateral bodies should be noted. Many of the Global South enterprises described above interact with governments and may receive revenues and other forms of direct support from them. Nonetheless, governments in general are not a key factor in starting and building the most successful of these enterprises – those that have achieved the greatest scale to date. This is congruent with the technology/entrepreneur model, from which these early success stories derive, in terms of the relatively minimal role of government in the success of such ventures.

Can conventional government aid programs and philanthropic capital sources be adapted to fit into the emerging approach of funding technology/entrepreneurs in the South? Chapter 8 explores this topic in depth. In the present context, the question is how to disaggregate existing programs into a series of funds that look like Acumen. University of Toronto law professor Michael Trebilcock has pointed out the need to find trusted intermediaries to help bypass the governments of developing nations as aid recipients.[20] One bold experiment is Grand Challenges Canada (see chapter 8), which represents 5 per cent of the foreign assistance budget of Canada's Department of Foreign Affairs, Trade and Development over its planned five-year initial phase.

More broadly, traditional forms of financing are beginning to align with entrepreneur-centric approaches. The Gates Foundation is experimenting with a range of such approaches, as evidenced in one example by the University of Toronto's participation in the Reinvent the Toilet Challenge – an initiative that uses the idea of lean start-ups and rapid prototyping. The Skoll Foundation is focused on social entrepreneurship. In the Acumen case, there are commercial VCs investing side by side with Acumen in some enterprises, creating blurred lines – some of the organizations being backed are for-profits and others are not-for-profits. One could reasonably expect broader participation by commercial VC firms in the future.

The innovation components discussed here will come together in unique ways in each setting. There will be a mixing of these types of models, with continual adjustment.

Sustainability – In Several Ways

An ongoing solution to the issues related to the precarious state of human life in the poorest areas in the Global South emphasizes notions of the sustainability of innovations and organizations – in the broadest sense of sustainability as well as in the narrower sense related to the environmental and carbon impact of their operations.

Christopher Kennedy and his team at the University of Toronto have developed detailed estimates of greenhouse gas emissions (GHGs) of major world cities, and the components of those emissions.[21] Their analysis estimates both gross emissions and per-capita emissions. Lorraine Sugar has extended that work to large emerging Chinese cities and cities in the developing world.[22] The Chinese cities are already on a par with North American and European cities in terms of per-capita emissions.

Dar es Salaam is at very low levels of emissions – one metric ton of CO^2 equivalent per capita per annum versus ten metric tons in China and twenty in colder North American cities such as Toronto and Denver. So Dar es Salaam is already at a desirable level from a sustainability perspective. The question is, can Dar es Salaam's GDP per capita grow by an order of magnitude while leaving the emissions level where it is? And can Toronto and Denver move to the level achieved by Dar es Salaam (Sugar's analysis would say that is unlikely, even with the most extreme conservation measures) while leaving GDP levels where they are? There are many approaches one could envision for the emerging city. Are mass transit systems the answer? Could you build more vertical cities? A recent study by McKinsey and Company addresses these issues in the case of emerging market cities, proposes an urban sustainability index, and indicates broad areas where solutions may lie.[23]

Moving to a broader view of sustainability, how does an ongoing infrastructure to support innovation in the Global South develop? Examples of a number of innovative organizations in the Global South have been cited earlier. They may develop without or with the support of hybrid value chain partners, including financing sources, from the North. The "crowd sourcing" approaches developed by the Kenyan software enterprise Ushahidi have come into wide use in Africa and elsewhere in the South with little outside prompting. Ushahidi may break out in the North as well as in the South, with success promoting the further use of such approaches in the North, including with disadvantaged populations such as those in North American inner cities. Is there any reason this could not be replicated in other application areas and in other segments? The Aravind Eye Care System's consulting arm, LAECO, has worked in many locations – notably excluding North America and Europe – to consult with local partners who are interested in local adoption of elements of the Aravind approach (as compared to wide-scale replication).[24] In some ways, bypassing the burdens and in some case failed approaches of the Global North – the ability to start with a clean slate and leapfrog – is a more attractive and productive route.

Interdisciplinary collaboration has a key role in the search for sustainable solutions. Creativity is required to construct innovative solutions to pressing issues, and a single approach – say a technology-centric viewpoint – will not work. All of the mechanisms required to envision, construct, finance, and manage systems of the hybrid form described here call for a diversity of inputs and perspectives.

A model of a networked global organization, a potential template for future organizations, comes from a possibly unlikely source – within the Canadian government. RETScreen International is an entrepreneurial organization that embodies the notions of sustainability, partnering, and global adaptation. RETScreen is a software package for designing renewable energy systems. The RETScreen system started as a Master's thesis by Gregory Leng, the leader of the RETScreen organization, and has gone from there to become a Canadian entrepreneurial success story. It is a highly collaborative tool, with innovative features that allow multiple users to work together on a specific project, working in the language of their choice – at present, thirty-five different languages. The RETScreen operation is run by a small staff of twelve, augmented by a global set of collaborators ranging from individual academics to NASA. The RETScreen software has been downloaded for free by 380,000 users to date and is very popular in Asia and in developing countries. And the organization behind this innovation is the Canmet Energy lab, a very small, very innovative, very entrepreneurial unit of the Canadian government.

Assuming the ability to combine business models, partners, and financing sources, one can envision the invention of new industries aimed at the Global South – and with individuals and organizations in the Global South as active participants in the process, along with hybrid value chain partners from the North. From there it is not difficult to envision organizations from the Global South – a cadre of Aravinds and Ushahidis – as active participants in their sectors globally.

In the specific case of the financing sources for these enterprises, as in all VC investing, some early successes will breed further experimentation and innovative approaches. It is perhaps too soon to point to any specific winners, but many portfolio companies of the BOP impact investment funds are scaling and, as a result, are significantly improving the lives of their customers. In all cases, there will be ongoing questions concerning the factors that lead to successful scaling – those that allow some approaches to succeed while other promising ideas and enterprises do not.

Conclusion

The construct of the technology entrepreneur has succeeded in the North through the early development of the closely matched financing mechanism of risk capital. The models for financing development in the Global South to date have generally looked very different, relying largely on government aid and the support of multilateral bodies, with the addition of some philanthropic capital from farsighted foundations. Bringing the financing mechanisms into place to support the technology/entrepreneur axis in the South will allow the latter to reach its full potential and to proliferate.

The opportunities for innovation in the networked global organization seem boundless, and the range of problems that can be addressed equally vast. The harnessing of human potential to address critical issues of global poverty is more tractable with these entrepreneur- and venture-centric approaches. To return to William Easterly's construct, many of us can be "searchers" – we can be part of this broad collaborative effort to define and propel forward these new approaches to innovation in development. Or, in the words of Bill Gates, speaking at Davos in 2008, "These are not a few isolated stories; this is a world-wide movement, and we all have the ability and the responsibility to accelerate it."

THE IDEA IN BRIEF

Many ventures launched by technology entrepreneurs have succeeded in the North because of the availability of the closely matched financing mechanism of entrepreneurial risk capital. Similar approaches are being adapted to fund global development enterprises, with new hybrid value delivery systems further supporting the approach.

IMPLICATIONS

1 A new breed of financing mechanisms is becoming available to assist small enterprises in the Global South, both for-profits and not-for-profits.
2 The magnitude of the need for financing can be mitigated through such enterprises' leadership of or participation in strategically designed hybrid value chains (consisting in a specific case of some combination of one or more MNCs, government bodies and multilateral organizations, and other small enterprises and organizations) that greatly amplify their efforts and allow for scaling
3 These mechanisms will lead to the proliferation and potential success of a wide range of small enterprises working on multiple fronts to address many of the key challenges in the Global South, resulting in a "world-wide movement."

FOOD FOR THOUGHT

What needs to be done so that success and growth lead to a more sustainable – not less sustainable – environment in the developing world?

REFERENCES

1 Easterly, W. (2007). *The white man's burden: Why the West's efforts to aid the rest have done so much ill and so little good*. New York: Penguin Press.
2 Bornstein, D. (2007). *How to change the world: Social entrepreneurs and the power of new ideas*. Revised Edition. Oxford: Oxford University Press.
3 Prahalad, C.K., & Hart, S.L. (2002). "The fortune at the bottom of the pyramid." *Strategy + Business* 26.
4 Atsmon, Y., Child, P., Dobbs, R., & Narasimhan, L. (2012). "Winning the $30 trillion decathlon: Going for gold in emerging markets." *McKinsey Quarterly* 4: 20–35.
5 Prahalad & Hart (2002), "The fortune at the bottom of the pyramid."
6 Ibid.
7 Juma, C., & Yee-Cheong, L. (2005). *Innovation: Applying knowledge in development*. U.N. Millennium Report: Task Force on Science, Technology, and Innovation.
8 Jacobson, M. (2009). "Review of solutions to global warming, air pollution, and energy security." *Energy and Environmental Science* 2: 148–73.
9 Sargent, T. (2005). *The dance of molecules: How nanotechnology is changing our lives*. Toronto: Viking Canada.
10 Rogers, E. (1962). *Diffusion of innovations*. New York: Free Press.
11 Juma & Yee-Cheong (2005), *Innovation*.
12 Friedman, T. (2005) *The world is flat: A brief history of the twenty-first century*. New York: Farrar, Straus and Giroux.
13 Polak, P. (2008). *Out of poverty: What works when traditional approaches fail*. San Francisco: Berrett-Koehler Publishers.
14 McClanahan, P. (2012). "Impact bond model turns project funding on its head." *The Guardian* (27 December). Retrieved from: http://www.guardian.co.uk/.
15 Smil, V. (2010). *Energy transitions: History, requirements, prospects*. Santa Barbara, CA: Praeger.
16 Bhattacharyya, O., Khar, S., McGahan, A., Dunne, D., Daar, A., & Singer, P. (2010). "Innovative health service delivery models in low and middle income countries: What can we learn from the private sector?" *Health Research Policy and Systems* 8 (15 July): 24.

17 Drayton, B., & Budinich, V. (2010). "A new alliance for global change." *Harvard Business Review* (September).

18 Hystra & Ashoka. (2009). *Access to energy for the base of the pyramid.* (October).

19 Drayton & Budinich (2010), "A new alliance for global change," 4.

20 Trebilcock, M. (2010). "Why foreign aid mostly fails." University of Toronto Faculty of Law Working Paper. Retrieved from: http://www.law.utoronto .ca/documents/trebilcock/ForeignAid.pdf.

21 Kennedy, C., Steinberger, J., Gasson, B., Hansen, Y., Hillman, T., Havránek, M., et. al. (2009). "Greenhouse gas emissions from global cities." *Environmental Science & Technology* 43: 7297–302.

22 Sugar, L., Kennedy, C., & Hoornweg, D. (2012). "Synergies between climate adaptation and mitigation in development: Case studies of Amman, Jakarta, and Dar es Salaam." *International Journal of Climate Change Strategies and Management* 5 (1): 96–111.

23 Bouton, S., Lindsay, M., & Woetzel, J. (2012). "New models for sustainable growth in emerging-market cities." *McKinsey on Sustainability & Resource Productivity* (Summer): 54–63.

24 Soman, D., Kumar, V., Metcalfe, M., & Wong, J. (2012). "Beyond great ideas: A framework for scaling-up local innovation." *Rotman Magazine* (September).

8

Innovation and Foreign Policy

JANICE GROSS STEIN

Introduction

Established ways of doing business in development assistance will not be good enough. Development assistance faces three fundamental challenges. First, development assistance has targeted the poorest of the poor, the bottom billion, those at the bottom of the pyramid.[1] Today, the majority of the world's poor no longer live in poor countries. They are primarily in middle-income countries that generally neither receive nor want development assistance. Second, from the time they first became important tools of statecraft fifty years ago, development agencies have shifted the focus of their assistance. Finally, the structure and form have changed: development assistance is no longer a state monopoly but rather a partnered activity in a field crowded with non-governmental organizations, foundations, and the private sector. These three factors create fundamentally new challenges for the overseas development assistance programs that many rich countries continue to mount. I look at each of these trends in turn before examining the consequences for development assistance.

First and most important, the majority of poor people in the world today no longer live in poor countries. This is a striking change in a very short period of time. In 1990, 93 per cent of the world's poor lived in low-income or poor countries. Twenty years later, more than 70 per cent live in middle-income countries that are generally stable. Only about 23 per cent of the world's poor live in fragile and conflict-affected states, and they are divided among fragile low-income and middle-income societies.[2]

The sizzling growth rates in the economies of China and India have lifted more people out of poverty than the total of all development assistance of the last three decades, yet these same two countries together are home to a large number of the world's poor. In 1999, China graduated to middle-income status, as did Indonesia in 2003, India in 2007, and Nigeria and Pakistan in 2008. China was classified as upper middle income in 2011. What is striking is the concentration of the majority of the world's poor in a relatively few middle-income countries: about 60 per cent of the world's poor today live in China, India, Pakistan, Nigeria, and Indonesia. China and India do not accept any government-to-government development assistance and, indeed, both are now donor countries.

There is a lively debate about whether this dramatic shift will continue into the future. A new study projects that by 2025 most of the world's poor will again live in low-income countries.[3] Why? As middle incomes continue to grow, they will continue to lift people out of poverty. The poor continue to grow in what development experts label "fragile and conflict-affected states (FRACAS)" so that the majority of the world's poor will again be in poor countries. Part of the controversy is about labelling; some fragile states – Iraq, Nigeria, Pakistan – are large middle-income countries. Approximately 200 million poor people are counted differently in the two studies and this explains some but not all of the discrepancy in the projections. Even when these differences are removed, however, the first group still continues to project that by 2025 at least 60 per cent of the world's poor will be in middle-income countries. This pattern has significant implications for development assistance programs: Development agencies can continue to work in low-income and fragile states, knowing that, at best, they will reach fewer than half of the world's poor. When the global economy begins to experience robust and sustained growth again, it is likely that some of these low-income countries will move up the ladder. An exclusive focus on low-income countries will make overseas development assistance less and less relevant.

What kinds of changes in development assistance will be necessary? Development experts will have to put greater emphasis on sustainable economic development as they recognize the role of job creation in lifting people out of poverty. Economic development has not been the focus of development agencies for the last several decades. Programming to jump start or enhance economic development is far from straightforward, and a sizzling debate has erupted. I return to that debate in the second half of this chapter.

Agencies will need a new understanding of poverty for the majority of the world's poor. Issues of inclusion and redistribution will become far more important – and contentious – if donors feel that they have something to say about the domestic policies of middle-income countries. The private sector will become partners in development, foreign direct investment and remittances will continue to grow relative to development assistance, trade will matter as these countries demand better and fairer access to the markets of the rich, and middle-income governments will want consistency and coherence across all these sectors. All of this will create new political tensions and political challenges as middle-income countries insist on engaging on an equal basis as development partners rather than aid recipients.

The second change is the shifting focus of most development programs. In the last five decades, development agencies have experimented with different strategies in an effort to lift people out of poverty. Initially, governments focused their assistance on the development of infrastructure, helping to build roads, ports, and dams so that poor countries could begin to grow their economies. The results were disappointing. Bridges were built, but development did not "take off." They then shifted focus to building human capital and invested heavily in health, literacy, and social programs. That was quickly supplemented by programs that paid particular attention to women and girls as multipliers of development. Within a few years, development assistance focused on good governance, the rule of law, and improving systems of public finance in an effort to fight the corruption and misallocation of aid that critics of aid had begun to excoriate.

In the last decade, development agencies have recognized that there is no single "magic bullet" that will propel development forward, especially in very poor countries. Spurred by the Millennium Development Goals, the best development agencies have focused on integrating their development programming across sectors and on coordinating activities among donors, who often bumped up against one another, causing traffic jams and incoherence. These coordinated programs all use female empowerment and environmental sustainability as screens for everything they do. Unfortunately, coherence is often in the eye of the beholder, and coordinating is hardly a rallying cry to build support for development assistance in a world that is changing so dramatically. Now, governments are turning the focus of their development assistance once again, this time to economic development.

Finally, not only the focus of development assistance but also the structure of programs and the form of program delivery have changed. When overseas development assistance began fifty years ago, national agencies found themselves working virtually alone in the field, bumping up occasionally against United Nations' agencies and more often against religious organizations that had long had a missionary presence on the ground. Fifty years later, the field is crowded with non-governmental organizations, strengthened religious organizations coming from many traditions, foundations, and not-for-profit and for-profit micro-credit institutions. In a remarkable change, development agencies today rarely deliver assistance on the ground and have a limited presence in the field. They contract out programming to national non-governmental agencies, multilateral institutions, international financial institutions, and local civil society organizations. Development agencies set objectives, contract partners, and demand performance metrics and accountability for results.[4] They are now managers rather than "doers." To use the language of new public management, they steer rather than row the boat. Despite all the change, performance is mixed. One study recently estimated that about 65 per cent of overseas development spending assistance still does not reach its targets. Only 35 per cent is spent in the local economy, and an astonishingly small 1 per cent is channelled through the local private sector to small and medium-sized businesses that create jobs.[5] Even more striking, aid is now dwarfed by foreign investment and by remittances from nationals who have migrated to seek better opportunity and send money home to help their families. Again, a comparison is striking: fifty years ago, development assistance constituted about 70 per cent of capital inflows into poor countries; today, the estimate is that aid accounts for only about 13 per cent. In short, development assistance is today less important in the total envelope of capital inflows and, as we shall see, less able than ever to reach the majority of the world's poor.

The context today of overseas development assistance is dramatically different than it was even a decade ago. To put the challenge bluntly, *the majority of the poor live in middle-income countries and development assistance accounts for only 13 per cent of capital flows to poor countries.* In this radically altered context, I consider how development assistance agencies can enhance the prospects of one important dimension of economic development – innovation – that benefits the poor in the economies of lower- and middle-income countries.

Frugal Innovation

In a tightly integrated global economy, innovation is increasingly important as a wealth generator. I focus on inclusive growth and innovation that reduce poverty, create employment opportunities for the poor, and increase access to essential services in health and education that the poor generally do not have access to. When inclusive growth connects poor individuals and communities with opportunities that foster social and economic growth, it diminishes the trade-offs between growth and equality.[6] Inclusive growth is the official policy of India, and it is no surprise, therefore, that the term "frugal innovation" is often used to describe inclusive innovation in India. Indians live in a culture of *"jugaad,"* where, *force majeure*, they develop makeshift but workable solutions from limited resources.[7] *"Jugaad* is about innovation," Tharoor argues. "It is about finding inexpensive solutions, often improvised on the fly, within the constraints of a resource-starved developing country full of poor people. An Indian villager constructs a makeshift vehicle to transport his livestock and goods by rigging a wooden cart with an irrigation hand pump that serves as an engine. That's *jugaad.*"[8] We know more about the supply side of frugal innovation than we do about the demand. Indian companies have long recognized the opportunities in meeting previously overlooked demand at the "bottom of the pyramid." On the supply side, simplifying and *scaling down* is at the centre of frugal innovation, or innovating for the poor. Frugal innovation is often led by the private sector, looking for new markets that can grow based on large volumes of consumers. The Tata Nano, priced at $2,500, is stripped of all the luxuries and fripperies that are standard in the cars manufactured in the developed world. Stripping away anything that is unnecessary certainly enables the manufacturer to lower the price. But the Nano is not only about stripping away what others have done. Tata innovated. It reduced the use of steel by inventing an aluminum engine, increased space by moving the wheels to the edge of the chassis, and relied on a modular design that enables the car to be assembled from kits.[9] I return to the story of the Nano when I consider the demand side of innovation – which may prove to be as challenging as the innovation of the product itself.

India is now a world leader in the frugal innovation of health-care diagnostics. Supplying medical devices through frugal innovation has enormous potential to change the access of the poor to health-care services. Indian manufactures have developed the GE MAC 400, a hand-held electrocardiogram (ECG) device that costs less than half of the cheapest available alternative. The GE MAC 400 comes with a tiny portable printer, making it small enough to fit into a knapsack and run on batteries; it has reduced the cost of an ECG to just $1 per patient.[10] Some five million Indians die of cardiovascular diseases every year, more than a quarter of them under sixty-five years old. Reducing the cost so significantly should greatly increase the capacity of the Indian government to provide cardiac diagnostics to the poorest of the poor. An Indian company has invented a cheaper hepatitis B vaccine, bringing down the price from $15 per injection to about ten cents. Insulin's price has fallen by 40 per cent, thanks to India's leading biotech firm. A Bangalore company's diagnostic tool to test for tuberculosis and infectious diseases costs $200, compared to $10,000 for comparable equipment in the West. It is an unanticipated but potentially very significant benefit of innovating for the poor that this kind of frugal innovation is now of increasing interest in the developed world as governments face austerity, shrinking budgets, and escalating health-care costs.

The story of the Nano as an innovation for the poor becomes more challenging when we move beyond the design and production of an innovative product to the poor as consumers – the demand side of innovation. The Nano has not yet found its market: those who have been pulled out of poverty and joined the middle class seem to have grander ambitions about the kind of car they want and therefore do not choose to buy a Nano; it would not adequately reflect their new status. Yet for the large number of poor and very poor, the price of the Nano is still too high. The same issue will be relevant as medical devices and point-of-care diagnostics come to market at prices that make these services affordable even to the poor. Policy makers will have to understand much better than they do now when, why, and how the poor will access these services. Are there cultural, communal, or individual obstacles to successful adoption? How is the "last mile" problem addressed, the challenge of bringing innovation to poor consumers who are not centrally located or easily reached? Who are the "credible" distributors at the end of the road who can vouch for the value of an innovative product or service?

At the forefront of the agenda of inclusive growth and frugal innovation are the poor as consumers. Thinking of the poor as valuable consumers is itself an important conceptual innovation, with profound implications for policy. When working with the poor is considered part of corporate social responsibility, for example, poor communities generally remain to the side, apart from the DNA of corporate activities. Thinking of the poor as consumers puts them squarely at the heart of the enterprise, worthy of the attention of strategists, product designers and developers, and marketers. Thinking of the poor as consumers puts them at the centre of development assistance. We need to understand why poor consumers use very scarce resources to buy products and then how they use these products or services. Not all consumption, of course, reduces poverty. Some products that consume scarce resources may provide very limited benefit while others – such as smart phones that transmit crop data in real time and allow diagnostic testing for diabetes – can have significant impact. Microfinance, for example, can increase indebtedness under some conditions.[11] What impact does product use have on social and economic well-being? Bradley finds that financial capital alone is not enough to reduce poverty; innovative products and practices are essential to change outcomes.[12] These findings are a cautionary tale to economic development and social entrepreneurship models that focus exclusively on increasing the supply of capital to resource-constrained communities.

The poor are not only consumers in processes of frugal innovation. They are also innovators – and owners and governors of innovation. The Indian villager who constructed the makeshift cart and attached it to a hand pump is an innovator. An infinite number of such innovations are generated routinely in poor communities as they struggle to adapt, but they are invisible to those outside, who see only the poverty and not the innovation. "Bricolage" describes how individuals innovate and improvise by recombining existing but less useful resources to add value through reconstruction and recombination.[13] The concept of bricolage can be adapted to environments with very few resources to help explain how individuals improvise and create value. I argue that at the core of the next phase of development will be the poor as consumers and as innovators.

Inclusive innovation is the development and implementation of new products, services, and processes that enhance the social and economic well-being of the poor who are disenfranchised within their own communities.[14] We do not know a great deal about the causes of inclusive innovation – about the conditions that enable the development of new or recombinant ideas or institutions. Nor do we know with confidence why some succeed and others fail. We know even less about the poor as consumers of innovation: when and why they adopt, use, and participate in innovative products, services, and processes. We need to understand the practices of innovation much better than we currently do. Finally, and most directly relevant to development assistance strategies, we do not yet have robust knowledge about the difference that policies and practices at all levels – in government, the private sector, and the large not-for-profit sector – can make.

Frugal Innovation and Government Policy

Little attention has been paid to the consequences of innovation policy. We do know that governments have usually been blind to the distributive consequences when they consider policy on innovation. It is simply not a screen that governments use when they consider how they can accelerate innovation. Yet governments, through their policies, can shape the environment of innovation. What are innovation policies? They are the laws, new institutions, organizations, regulations, and practices designed to encourage the development of innovative outputs.[15]

The critical political questions become: how can governments explain that part of their development assistance will explicitly be built on five- or ten-year horizons; and how can governments inculcate an understanding of and respect for the "smart failures" that are integral to innovation and inclusive growth? I conceive of "smart failures" as failures that do not result from factors that could have been anticipated – that are well known and therefore could have been avoided. Rather, "smart failures" result from novel interaction effects that could not have been anticipated, from the identification of new drivers, or from the adaptation of new products and processes to different environments. Successful innovators diagnose these causes of failure, learn, adapt, improve, and launch a new round in iterative processes of trial-and-error innovation. Without this kind of continuous learning, innovation is unlikely to succeed. Not all failures are smart – some should not occur at all because the causes of failure could have been anticipated in the early stages of design; but almost all failures can be made "smarter" by careful processes of diagnosis followed by quality improvements.

Development Assistance, Innovation, and Inclusive Growth

Donor countries are increasingly turning their attention to promoting economic development. At a meeting in Busan in 2011 on the effectiveness of aid, participants emphasized the importance of increased private sector participation in development. They agreed to ensure a "sound policy and regulatory environment for private sector development, increased foreign direct investment, public-private partnerships ... enable the participation of the private sector in the design and implementation of development policies and strategies ... [and] advance both development and business outcomes so that they are mutually reinforcing."[16]

It is important to distinguish sharply between "private sector development" – the development of the private sector in poor and lower-middle-income countries to encourage productive activities and job creation – and the "private sector *for* development" – enlisting the international private sector to achieve development goals and to leverage private sector finance for development objectives.[17] Participants at the Busan meeting emphasized both, at times interchangeably. Their call for better regulatory environments in developing countries emphasized local private sector development. There was an even stronger emphasis, however, on the private sector *for* development, on partnering with the international private sector and encouraging private sector actors to make investments in developing countries by reducing and sharing risk. Typically, governments partner through challenge funds for foreign direct investment, loan guarantees, grants, and subsidies.[18] Donor governments also seek to leverage private sector finance through public-private sector partnerships, portfolio investments, and the creation of private funds backed by government guarantees. The European Commission, for example, committed to "leveraging private sector activity and resources for delivering public goods."[19]

The shift to partnering and risk sharing with the private sector is partly due to the visible and impressive results of economic growth in China and India on poverty reduction. Donors have visible, confirming evidence of the impact of economic growth on lifting people out of poverty. Experts argue that while economic growth is not sufficient for poverty reduction, it is certainly necessary. And not any kind of economic growth will do. To reduce poverty, growth must be accompanied by a transition towards higher productivity and employment creation; it is growth in jobs that leads to increases in incomes and demand, the expansion of goods and services, and the broadening of the tax base that can finance public goods for those who are still at the bottom.[20]

None of these strategies are without risk. Development agencies are not interested in funding economic growth; their objective is economic transformation or inclusive growth. There is no consensus on the strategies to promote inclusive growth: is it increasing employment opportunities for all, or supporting linkage programs between international and local enterprises, or supporting "bottom of the pyramid" businesses targeted at local consumers?[21] There are almost certainly trade-offs among these policy choices, especially in an environment where capital is constrained and resources are scarce. These trade-offs reflect a more fundamental issue: "What is required for a private sector investment to be considered developmental?" the European Commission asked. "At what point is it simply business and at what point should it attract public money in the form of donor support …?"[22] These are not easy questions, and the potential is high for the misuse of funds, the capture of programs, and corruption.

The answer lies partly in concepts of inclusive business and inclusive innovation. "Inclusive business entails creating a net positive development impact through a financially profitable business model."[23] Four types of businesses can be considered inclusive: commercial businesses that sell goods and services that are needed by the poor and have significant development impact; companies that have a significant impact on poverty and attempt to increase that impact through innovation; commercial small and medium-sized companies that operate in the local economy and wish to grow their companies and create employment; and social enterprises that use market mechanisms and commercial models of delivery.[24] The challenge for donors is to support inclusive business and innovation without unnecessary subsidies or financing what companies would want to do and be able to do without outside financial help. Donors must be (reasonably) confident that they are adding value through their funding to inclusive growth and job creation. In short, development assistance needs to focus on long horizons, smart failures, openness to entrepreneurial and innovative cultures, and governance that gives voice to the poor as innovators, owners, and consumers.

What do we know about government experiments with investment funds that promote innovation? Canada is leading an important experiment through Grand Challenges Canada. Located at the Sandra Rotman Centre at the University of Toronto and University Health Network, the program is funded by the federal government for a five-year term, so it escapes the absurdities of an annual audit of "value-for-money" that is so disruptive of innovation processes. It will offer five challenges to researchers in the South, inviting proposals for "frugal" and "innovative" solutions to point-of-care diagnostics that can improve health care delivered to hundreds of millions of people in the South. Grand

Challenges Canada is an extraordinary experiment, but so far it is stimulating innovation only at the very early stages of discovery. It has not yet tackled the difficult challenges of commercialization and sustainable scaling. Nor has it yet paid systematic attention to the poor as consumers, to the demand side of successful inclusive innovation.

There are experiments by other developed countries that could inform a development investment fund. One such model is Obviam that began as a fund *within* the Swiss government and has now been spun out. It is a Fund of Funds – it invests in independent funds in emerging markets. The fund is now managed by an arm's-length board, appointed by the Swiss government, and the board is accountable for the integrity of its processes and for its results. Results are measured not only by the traditional metric of return on investment (ROI) but also by the number of successful companies it has supported and the number of sustainable jobs these companies have created.

Obviam is one of the few investment advisers with a track record of more than ten years in emerging and frontier market private equity fund investments. It has focused exclusively on emerging markets, diversifying globally into Africa, Asia, Eastern Europe, and Latin America, developing a wide network of relationships in these markets. In 2010, Obviam's predecessor, SIFEM, won the G-20 SME Challenge Award for innovative investment solutions to unlocking access to finance for small and medium-sized enterprises in developing countries. The long-term and hands-on nature of private equity is particularly attractive in these markets, where creating value through business improvements delivers significant value.

The Business Call to Action (BCtA) also has a significant track record. Supported by a number of donors, the BCtA works with businesses to develop inclusive models and to "engage low-income citizens as consumers, producers, suppliers, and distributors of goods and services."[25] The Business Call to Action works with forty-five companies and provides advice and assistance in their development activities, which target job creation, the provision of financial services to the poor, and improving access to clean water.

Development Assistance and Inclusive Innovation: What Can Governments Do?

Governments can help enable inclusive growth and innovation by building enabling platforms through their overseas development assistance programs. For example,

1 Governments can create a Development Investment Fund. Governments can wall off a significant part of the overseas development assistant (ODA) envelope and create a separate agency to stimulate innovation through competitive processes. Grand Challenges Canada is now partnered with the Gates Foundation and draws on its networks to broaden its reach.

2 Governments can create a Private Sector Investment Program that enables public-private partnerships to meet development objectives. The Netherlands has created such a fund, which provides grants to partnerships between Dutch companies and those from developing countries. This kind of program can also fund local companies in partnerships with local governments, although donor governments have generally not been consulted or engaged as partners.[26] The Private Infrastructure Development Group (PIDG), a multi-donor organization, has set up facilities that provide a wide range of support to the development of infrastructure and job creation.

3 Governments can fund entrepreneurship and mentorship programs. In Canada, a private sector entrepreneur has created The Next 36 to help launch the careers of Canada's most promising and innovative undergraduates. The program identifies these students through a rigorous national selection process and gives them the academic foundation, practical skills, role models, and networks to become Canada's next generation of entrepreneurial leaders. Development assistance programs can seek out bright young people from poor societies, invest in training in entrepreneurship in partnership with the educational sector and the private sector, both in the South and at home, and invite private sector leaders to mentor these promising young people and to invest in providing capital at different stages of the innovation process.

4 Governments can partner with local businesses and non-governmental agencies to understand better the demand side of innovation. What enables adoption in different communities? What impedes adoption? What characteristics of product and process increase adoption rates? And what impact do these innovations have on reducing poverty once they are adopted?

5 Governments can provide "one-stop shopping" centres for governments and private sector leaders from the South who seek to create enabling environments for innovation. They can help to educate public officials about regulatory requirements, capital markets, and the design of programs that enable innovation.

6 Governments can create investment funds that can be used to invest in promising middle-stage innovation, in partnership with local investors in the South. The expectation of success cannot be higher than in the private sector, which is usually no better than 5 to 10 per cent. Here is where the education of the public and the management of expectations are critical.

The metrics of success are among the most controversial issues in development assistance. It seems obvious that governments should measure and evaluate the success of the programs they fund, and learn from their failures. Yet measurement is a multiple-edged sword. What is easy to measure can drive spending and programming as governments looks for "results" that they can advertise to their publics. Programs that focus on vaccination or enrolment in schools take precedence over more complex measures to improve public health and educational outcomes. A turn from the "inputs" to the "outcomes" of development programs is a distinct improvement, but the larger problems remain. Work on good governance, generally recognized as one essential driver of development, is unlikely to fit neatly into any outcomes-based metric.

A vast literature on the metrics of success and an industry of consultants who go out into the field to evaluate programs have grown up in the last two decades, at an enormous cost. The cost is not only financial. Frequent measurement and evaluation have often hobbled innovation in development programs, stifled risk taking, prevented long-term commitments, and shut down creativity. Governments are struggling to find better ways to measure results, ways that are sensitive to the complex interactions among the drivers of poverty, that have appropriate time horizons, and that do not stifle creativity.

A recent innovation in the financing and measuring of development programs is the social impact bond. Private investors fund a development intervention, which is designed by voluntary organizations working with government and is implemented by the voluntary organization that was involved in the design phase. Only if the program produces the agreed-upon benefits does the government pay the private investor a return on the original investment. Freed from the often onerous demands of reporting throughout a project, implementing agencies can focus on delivering results and better adapt to local circumstances.[27] Social impact bonds may be very useful when results are measurable and good data are available, but none of these programs captures the difficulty of evaluating programs of alleviating poverty that is embedded in complex economic, political, and cultural chains.

Business leaders express frustration with some of the bureaucratic procedures and concern about the constraints imposed by partnering with governments, and worry especially about their capacity to respond in a nimble and timely way to rapidly changing environments. Firms are also often unaware of available opportunities and sources of support.[28] Moreover, very few of these programs have yet been subjected to rigorous evaluation, and their multiplier effects have not been adequately measured.

More serious is the risk that these programs can be captured by business or that they fail to provide "development additionality," that is, they top up activities that businesses would have engaged in anyway. Norway's development agency has done an evaluation, and the results are discouraging. The review concludes that its partnership program was not effective in promoting trade and addressing the economic marginalization of poor countries.[29] It seems that the greatest beneficiaries have been Norwegian firms. As they move forward, governments will need to find an appropriate balance of risk between public and private partners. Clearly, private sector interests and development objectives can and should be aligned, but monitoring and evaluating that alignment and assessing value for money continue to present significant challenges. Evidence about outcomes is thin, and many of these programs do not yet have an established track record of performance and results.

To reach the majority of the world's poor, governments will have to redesign and repurpose some of their development assistance programs over the next decade to emphasize the creation of opportunity and employment among the poor, who now live not only in poor countries but predominantly in middle-income countries. An important part of that story will be to enable inclusive innovation that is appropriate to Southern markets, builds on knowledge of local markets and local preferences, enables triple-bottom-line enterprises, and nurtures entrepreneurship and innovation among young leaders. Governments will need to create new instruments that can operate across silos and in partnership with the private sector, to have a higher tolerance for smart failures, and to think differently about risk. These are very different challenges from those that development assistance programs have faced in the past.

THE IDEA IN BRIEF

Implications for Development Assistance Programs
1 Enable inclusive innovation that builds on knowledge of local markets and local preferences.
2 Nurture entrepreneurship and innovation among young leaders.
3 Partner with the private sector and increase tolerance for "smart" failures.

FOOD FOR THOUGHT

Governments will have to redesign and repurpose some of their development assistance programs over the next decade to emphasize the creation of opportunity and employment among the poor, who now live not only in poor countries but predominantly in middle-income countries.

REFERENCES

1 Collier, P. (2007). *The bottom billion: Why the poorest countries are failing and what can be done about it.* Oxford: Oxford University Press.
2 Sumner, A. (2011). *Poverty in middle-income countries.* Bellagio Summary. Brighton: Institute of Development Studies. Retrieved 18 June 2012 from: http://www.bellagioinitiative.org/wp-content/uploads/2011/10/Poverty_in_middleincome_countries_BS.pdf.
3 Kharas, H., & Rogerson, A. (2012). *Horizon, 2025: Creative destruction in the aid industry.* London: Overseas Development Institute (ODI).
4 Stein, J. Gross. (2008). "Humanitarian organisations: Accountable why, to whom, for what, and how?" In Michael Barnett & Thomas Weiss (Eds), *Contemporary humanitarianism in global and theoretical perspective.* Ithaca, NY: Cornell University Press.
5 Building Markets. (2012). *Aid isn't ending poverty. Mining is.* Ottawa.
6 For a discussion of "inclusive innovation," see George, G., McGahan, A., & Prabhu, J. (2012). "Innovation for inclusive growth: Towards a theoretical framework and research agenda." *Journal of Management Studies* 49: 661–83.
7 See Radjou, N., Prabhu, J., & Ahuja, S. (2012). *Jugaad innovation: Think frugal, be flexible, generate breakthrough growth.* San Francisco: Jossey-Bass; Gulati, R. (2010). "Management lessons from the edge." *Academy of Management*

Perspectives 24 (2): 25–7; and Krishnan, R. (2010). *From jugaad to systematic innovation*. Bangalore: Utpreraka Foundation.

8 See Tharoor, S. (2012). "India's frugal revolution." *Globe and Mail* (16 July). Retrieved 18 July 2012 from: http://www.theglobeandmail.com /commentary/indias-frugal-revolution/article4415917.

9 Ibid.

10 Ibid.

11 See Banerjee, A., & Duflo, E. (2011). *Poor economics: A radical rethinking of the way to fight global poverty*. New York: Public Affairs.

12 Bradley, S.W., McMullen, J.S., Artz, K., & Simiyu, E.M. (2012). "Capital is not enough: Innovation in developing economies." *Journal of Management Studies* 49 (4) (June): 684–718.

13 Baker, T., & Nelson, R. (2005). "Creating something from nothing: Resource construction through entrepreneurial bricolage." *Administrative Science Quarterly* 50 (3) (September): 329–66.

14 See George, McGahan, and Prabhu (2012), "Innovation for inclusive growth."

15 Breznitz, D., & Zahavi, A. (2012). "Having our cake and eating it too? Inequality and innovation policy: Benefiting growth and minimizing negative externalities." Unpublished paper (July).

16 See 4th High Level Forum on Aid Effectiveness. (2011). Busan Partnership for Effective Development Co-operation. Busan, Republic of Korea, 29 November–1 December. Retrieved 5 October 2011 from: http://www .aideffectiveness.org/busanhlf4/images/stories/hlf4/OUTCOME _DOCUMENT_FINAL_EN.pdf. That site has now been replaced by www.effectivecooperation.org (retrieved 5 August 2013).

17 Byiers, B., & Rosengren, A. (2012). "Common or conflicting interests? Reflections on the private sector (for) development agenda." *European Centre for Development Policy Management (ECDPM)* 131 (July). Retrieved 8 January 2013 from: http://www.ecdpm.org/Web_ECDPM/Web/Content /Navigation.nsf/index2?readform&http://www.ecdpm.org/Web_ECDPM /Web/Content/Content.nsf/0/29847B4E6EF505C0C1257A3200751283?O penDocument

18 Kwakkenbos, J. (2012). "Private profit for public good? Can investing in private companies deliver for the poor?" Eurodad, European Network on Debt and Development. Retrieved 10 January 2013 from: http://eurodad .org/wp-content/uploads/2012/05/Private-Profit-for-Public-Good.pdf; and Perry, G. (2011). "Growing business or development priority? Multilateral development banks' direct support to private firms." Center for Global Development. Retrieved 10 January 2013 from: http://www.cgdev .org/files/1424992_file_Perry_MDB_Direct_Support_FINAL.PDF.

19 European Commission. (2011). "Increasing the impact of EU development policy: An agenda for change." Communication from the Commission to the European Parliament, the Council, the European Economic and Social Committee and the Committee of the Regions, COM(2011)702 final. Retrieved 8 December 2011 from: http://ec.europa.eu/europeaid/what/development-policies/documents/agenda_for_change_en.pdf.

20 Byiers and Rosengren (2012), "Common or conflicting interests," 16.

21 Kwakkenbos (2012), "Private profit for public good."

22 European Commission (2011), "Increasing the impact of EU development policy."

23 Wach, E. (2012). "Measuring the inclusivity of 'inclusive' business." IDS Practice Paper. Vol. 9. Institute of Development Studies, U.K. Retrieved 30 November 2012 from: http://www.ids.ac.uk/files/dmfile/Pp9.pdf.

24 Ashley, C. (2009). "Harnessing core business for development impact." ODI Background Note. Overseas Development Institute, London. Retrieved 8 January 2011 from: http://www.odi.org.uk/sites/odi.org.uk/files/odi-assets/publications-opinion-files/3566.pdf.

25 Business Call to Action (BCtA). (2010). "Innovation that improves lives," Web brochure. Retrieved 8 January 2011 from: http://www.businesscalltoaction.org/wp-content/uploads/2010/11/Business-Call-to-Action-Brochure-Web-Layout.pdf.

26 Kwakkenbos (2012), "Private profit for public good," 10.

27 http://www.theguardian.com/global-development/poverty-matters/2012/dec/27/impact-bond-model-project-funding. Retrieved 14 January 2013.

28 U.N. Global Compact. (2010). "Delivering results: Moving towards scale." Report on an inclusive business dialogue during the U.N. Summit on the Millennium Development Goals. (21 September). Retrieved 10 January 2011 from: http://www.unglobalcompact.org/docs/issues_doc/development/Delivering_Results_Moving_Towards_Scale.pdf.

29 Norad. (2010). "Evaluation of Norwegian business-related assistance main report." Norad Evaluation Department Report 3/2010, xvi. Retrieved 15 January 2011 from: http://www.norad.no/en/tools-and-publications/publications/publication?key=176080.

Inclusive Innovation

WILL MITCHELL
ANITA M. McGAHAN

The chapters in this book highlight the tension that arises when using supply-side insights to attempt to achieve demand-side opportunities for improving the health of people in the Global South and for lower-income populations throughout the world. Supply-side innovation focuses on designing new goods and services. By contrast, the demand side of innovation focuses on understanding the needs and values of people who might use the goods and services. Scalable innovation for the poor requires the linking of great design on the supply side with contextual relevance on the demand side. As a whole, the chapters in this book seek a synthesis that integrates the benefits of scalable technological advance with a deep understanding of user-oriented relevance.

Clearly, of course, innovative supply-side efforts by academics, companies, public and non-profit organizations, and thoughtful individuals to design new products and services or to adapt existing products and services are critically important for meeting the health-care and other development needs of lower-income populations throughout the world. Major supply-side opportunities exist in the realms of water, nutrition, sanitation, health support and treatment, and many other aspects of human health. Even now, though, many more potential innovations arise on the supply side – from individuals and organizations in both the Global North and the Global South – than succeed in achieving sustainable adoption on the demand side.

At the core, the key challenge today in improving global health is less a scarcity of supply-side insight and more a challenge of demand-side understanding. A common theme across the chapters is that potential innovators – whether they are creating new services or adapting existing goods for new uses – must engage with potential adopters and their environments to succeed in creating health and prosperity. This is a straightforward argument but one that is often lost when the excitement and narrowly focused activity of design and invention overwhelm the hard work and distributed scope involved in engaging with people in new social contexts.

Failure from the Supply Side Is Common – but There Are Pointers to Success on the Demand Side

The chapters in this book outline multiple examples of failed attempts to create health-care innovations in the Global South as a result of lack of demand-side understanding. Attempts to sell cheaper scaled-down versions of goods and services designed for developed markets often do not meet local needs. Well-intentioned attempts to create inexpensive food products, health-care services, and many other types of innovations often do not take account of local habits. Innovative activities often over-emphasize narrow economic incentives and under-emphasize behavioural norms and preferences that undo any apparent economic benefit. In general, many innovations fail because they are pushed by outside actors – sometimes from the Global North, at other times from high-level actors in local environments – rather than pulled from local needs and values. The examples of failed attempts will resonate with all readers who have participated in or observed efforts to improve health care throughout the world.

More strikingly, the discussions highlight initiatives that have succeeded in achieving sustainable adoption and begin to tease out factors that lead to success rather than failure. Joseph Wong (in chapter 1) underscores the importance of addressing time demands (e.g., travel, time from work) and social norms (e.g., trust, women working away from home). Dilip Soman (in chapter 2) emphasizes the importance of understanding behavioural incentives such as how people construct their perceptions of value, asymmetries in the impact of potential losses and potential gains, tendencies to stick with the status quo, lack of contextual understanding, overly complex information about potential innovations, lack of understanding of how people categorize their expenditures, and differences in time horizons. Yu-Ling Cheng and Beverly Bradley (in chapter 3) stress the importance of matching design to context and, where necessary, finding ways to adapt the context to the design (e.g., engaging in thoughtful initiatives around eating habits). Rahim Rezaie (in chapter 4) outlines the growing opportunities for innovations appropriate to poorer environments that may occur as traditional value chains become more disaggregated and increasingly add key players from China, India, Brazil, and other emerging markets. Anita McGahan, Rahim Rezaie, and Donald Cole (in chapter 5) develop the notion of "embedded innovation" that focuses on solidarity with the poor, collaboration in the field, sharing profits as well as risks, and increasing competition to serve the poor. Ashley Aimone Phillips, Nandita Perumal, Carmen Ho, and Stanley Zlotkin (in chapter 6) review studies of nutrition innovation, suggesting that key factors for success include appropriate design and cost effectiveness, local partnerships, community participation, and multi-sectoral involvement. Murray Metcalfe (in chapter 7) argues that key support for technical innovation needs to come via social capital, infrastructure development, and innovative business models such as hybrid value chains. Janice Stein (in chapter 8) argues that we need to develop approaches to frugal innovation that include sustainable economic development and recognize challenges of redistribution and equity that make it difficult to reach not only populations in lower-income countries but also the large body of the poor who live in middle- and upper-income countries.

Three Themes about the Demand Side of Innovation

Three themes cut through the examples and arguments about understanding the demand side of innovation: the need to address both the direct and supporting context, the need to understand contextual quality, and the growing importance of value chain integration.

The Context Involves both Direct and Supporting Factors

First, the chapters highlight the point that understanding the demand side requires recognizing both direct and supporting demand factors. Direct demand factors include the needs and values of focal users. Recognizing these is challenging, even for people and organizations located in a particular country, and is exponentially challenging for people who are based abroad. Yet, without the investment of time and effort to understand the relevant values of targeted users, even the most sophisticated and expensive supply innovations will fail.

Supporting factors on the demand side are even more complex. Supporting factors involve broader ecosystems that support the use of a new product or service. Such factors include family norms, distribution systems and other infrastructure, the engagement of government bodies and other social actors, and other parts of the relevant environment. Identifying such supporting factors is often even more difficult than the already challenging task of assessing focal value. Yet failing to engage the broader ecosystem will cause potentially viable innovations to fail.

Innovation Must Identify Contextual Quality

Second, the chapters imply the importance of recognizing "contextual quality" – that is, of innovating in ways that are relevant for the needs and contexts of particular users in LMIC environments rather than simply attempting to create cheap versions of goods and services that have succeeded in other contexts. Uncountable numbers of public, social, and corporate organizations have failed in efforts to bring health-care innovations to low-income settings because they viewed their task as providing cheap lower-quality goods and services "for the poor."

By contrast, successful innovations create goods and services that are not viewed as "cheap goods for the poor" but instead meet relevant needs and opportunities at a price that people with limited incomes (and/or the organizations that support them) can afford and are willing to pay. The notion of contextual quality recognizes that all people want high-quality goods – and, moreover, that they define quality not in some abstract way but in a way that meets their specific needs and values. This core recognition often facilitates the designing of affordable goods and services that eliminate unnecessary features that were relevant in higher-income contexts while emphasizing features that are highly relevant in a particular lower-income setting. Most generally, the notion of contextual quality is central to a demand-side perspective on innovation.

The idea of contextual quality has important implications for our understanding of where innovations are likely to occur. Historically, we have tended to view "major" innovation as characteristic of developed markets, with people and organizations in emerging markets engaging primarily in making incremental changes to goods and services designed for developed markets. By contrast, local actors in emerging markets are increasingly playing lead roles in major innovations that provide contextual quality appropriate to their environments. Examples range from high-quality eye and cardiac surgery in India to vaccines in Brazil to health insurance in South Africa. At the very least, contextual quality innovations by local players have growing potential to address local needs for health care. In the longer term, these innovative efforts have the potential to change the balance of both opportunity and power in global innovation and competition in the non-profit and commercial health-care sectors. Hence, the ideas in these chapters extend well beyond the focus on health care in the Global South.

Value Chain Integrators Create Value

Third, the chapters highlight the relevance of disaggregated value chains and, in turn, the growing importance of value chain integration. Disaggregated value chains arise when multiple independent actors undertake many of the key activities involved in developing, producing, selling, and supporting innovative activity. Such ecosystems stand in stark contrast to the traditional models of value chain organization, in which a few vertically integrated firms undertook specialized activities internally and outsourced more general components.

Commercial, public, and non-profit health-care activities throughout the world increasingly reflect the value chain context, both in the increased geographic scope of many of the activities and the increasing need for sophisticated skills that are beyond the resource base of any one organization. Examples arise in biopharmaceutical and medical device commercialization, health insurance, multilevel health care, nutrition development and commercialization, and many other goods and services relevant to health care and health support. The emphasis on disaggregated value chains highlights the recognition that successful innovation commonly requires changes throughout a constellation of activities provided by ecosystems of multiple actors. In parallel, "value chain integration" means innovating in ways that achieve meaningful coordination among the multiple corporate, public, and non-profit actors that are commonly involved in innovative efforts.

Within a successful value chain, one or more actors need to play lead roles as value chain integrators in coordinating activities throughout the ecosystem. Some value chains have a single primary integrator: in commercial settings, for instance, Apple functions as a value chain integrator for iPhones and iPads, while GlaxoSmithKline, Eli Lilly, and other major pharmaceutical companies function as value chain integrators in biopharma development and commercialization. In these examples, each value chain integrator undertakes some of the core development and/or commercialization activities and, even more importantly, identifies and coordinates strong partners to achieve successful commercial activity. Other value chains may have two or more firms acting as value chain integrators: in consumer electronics, for instance, Google and Samsung play complementary roles at the operating system and handset points along the smart phone value chain. In either case, though, a relatively small number of actors are key players in coordinating the activity of many firms, often very skilful specialized partners. In turn, successful value chain integrators in commercial settings commonly gain substantial profits from their success, owing to their coordinating skills.

The notion of value chain integration is just as important in creating successful health-care innovations in lower- and middle-income settings as it is in commercializing goods and services in higher-income locations. Indeed, the actors in health-care value chains involved in innovating for the poor are even more varied, commonly involving a mix of public research institutes and academic organizations, non-profit NGOs, public sector agencies, and commercial actors located in multiple countries. Each typically plays a critically important role in the value chain of innovation for the poor. Yet, if each works only independently, few practical innovations will emerge because of limited coordination. Hence, just as successful value chain integrators in commercial settings tend to be highly successful in terms of profitability, successful value chain integrators in social settings tend to be highly successful in leading social initiatives.

We are only beginning to come to grips with how to create and provide incentives for pro-poor health-care value chain integrators. Some examples arise when commercial actors recognize opportunities to create successful contextual quality along with relevant supporting infrastructure. One example is Cipla in India, which profitably provides biopharmaceutical and other medical-technical services in about 170 markets, including many very low-income countries. Some examples involve commercial partnerships: GlaxoSmithKline from the United Kingdom and Aspen from South Africa, for instance, are cooperating in the commercialization of medicines throughout Africa. Others involve public-private partnerships that seek to generate both private value and public impact: in the United States, the Centers for Disease Control and McKesson Corporation, for instance, have cooperated in vaccine targeting and distribution. Other examples involve efforts by foundations such as the Gates Foundation to coordinate the efforts of multiple global actors in vaccine development, health-care services, and other activities. Some involve public or quasi-public bodies, such as Fiocruz in Brasil, which plays a central role in coordinating the development and distribution of vaccines. Not-for-profit social organizations can also be effective value chain integrators: the Aravind Eye Care System in India, for instance, coordinates the activities of multiple players in support of the NGO's surgical services. Many other examples are starting to emerge, while there is even greater potential for innovative efforts to create new models of value chain integration that help health-care innovations reach targeted markets.

Again, the core theme of this book is that successful health-care innovation starts and ends with understanding the demand side of innovation adoption. Only with deep and thoughtful engagement with users and their environments will the most insightful supply-side initiatives have a sustainable impact. In turn, we are beginning to develop organizational models that bring together a wide variety of skills in order to match supply-side insights about contextual quality with demand-side opportunities.

Glossary

autonomy: The right to self-determination; self-governance; the right of individuals to make their own decisions.

behavioural economics: A field of social science that studies the behavioural antecedents of economic decision making at the individual level and its effects on the marketplace at an aggregate level.

beneficence: Concern to engage in actions that help others and/or help to prevent or remove harm.

bricolage: The construction/creation of new things or solutions from a variety of existing resources; adding value through reconstruction and recombination.

constraint-based innovation: An Indian term referring to improvisation to devise solutions where resources are limited. (*See also "jugaad."*)

defaults: In the context of decision making, a default refers to an implicit choice that the decision maker uses if she or he does not make an active choice.

development additionality: Private sector initiatives to add value to development outcomes beyond what would have been done in the normal course of doing business.

disaggregated value chain: A value chain that has broken up into its constituent parts.

disruptive innovation: An innovation that, in the process of creating a new market, disrupts an existing market or value network. For example, the emergence of on-demand Internet streaming media has disrupted business for traditional video stores.

double bottom line: An investment performance measure that includes both economic and social indicators. (*See also* "triple bottom line.")

entrepreneurial finance: The commercial sector disciplines and practices of venture capital investing (often in early-stage technology-driven companies) and buyout investing (in larger, well-established companies, often purchased through debt financing from third-party lenders as well as equity from investors).

formal labour: Types of jobs that employ workers on a full-time basis. Workers in the formal labour market are often eligible for firm-level or government-provided work-related benefits. (*See also* "informal labour.")

frugal innovation: Innovation that eliminates non-essential features that make a technology or service more costly to develop, manufacture, or market.

Gini coefficient: A statistical measure used to estimate the distribution of income (typically by household), with a score ranging from 0 to 1, where scores approaching 1.0 represent greater levels of inequality.

grassroots innovation: Efforts by specific communities to improve their living conditions through collective action.

hybrid value chain: A series of steps in conceptualizing a product and bringing it to market where the steps take place across enterprises and organizations and specifically involve a not-for- profit organization. Each organization performs one or more steps in the value chain.

informal labour: Casual, part-time, illegal, irregular, and seasonal forms of employment; employment for which few or no work-related benefits are provided by either firms or governments.

jugaad: A Hindi word used to describe a style of innovation that creatively uses available resources to solve a local problem; it is used to refer to the development of innovative solutions with scarce resources.

Keynesianism: The economic theory attributed to John Maynard Keynes which contends that intentional government stimulus (i.e., stimulus spending) can mitigate the effects of macro-economic cycles, specifically when economies are on a downswing.

neglected diseases: Diseases that are prevalent among economically impoverished and marginalized populations in the developing world but for which effective preventive or treatment solutions are not available because of lack of attention to developing solutions for them.

non-maleficence: Concern to ensure that one's actions "do no harm."

nudge/choice architecture: Design that guides a decision maker towards a particular option without the use of restrictions and attempts at active persuasion. The term "nudge" was made popular by a book of the same title by Richard Thaler and Cass Sunstein.

prospect theory: A theory that establishes the relationship between actual quantities of outcome (typically money) and the emotional outcomes associated with these. Prospect theory is one of the foundations of the behavioural approach to economics.

reverse innovation: The process by which innovations that are first developed in low- or middle-income nations subsequently find a market in high-income nations.

scaling down: Innovating to provide products and services for consumers with low incomes by simplifying the products and services and/or stripping away their unnecessary elements.

"smart" failures: Failures that result from novel interaction effects that could not have been anticipated, from the identification of new drivers, or from the adaptation of new products and processes to different environments. Successful innovators diagnose these causes of failure, learn, adapt, improve, and launch a new round in iterative processes of trial-and-error innovation.

triple bottom line: An investment performance measure that includes economic, social, and environmental indicators. (*See also* "double bottom line.")

user-centred innovation: Innovation based on understanding the needs of users through comprehensive analysis of their behaviour.

value chain: The series of processes and internal organizations that start with market intelligence and product conceptualization and progress through engineering, production, marketing, pricing, distribution, and delivery to the end customer. A value chain usually would be located inside a single enterprise, such as a multinational corporation.

value proposition: The promise of value to the consumer or user.

About the Contributors

Beverly Bradley is a PhD student in the Centre for Global Engineering at the University of Toronto. Combining her previous degrees in systems design and biomedical engineering from the University of Waterloo and Carleton University, Bev is interested in how a systems-thinking approach and techniques from the field of operations research can be applied to improve the effective and efficient use of medical technologies in low-income countries. For her PhD research, she applies these concepts to the issue of poor and inadequate medical oxygen systems for treating illnesses such as childhood pneumonia. Her country of focus is The Gambia, West Africa, where she has spent more than a year living and doing research since 2009. Bev has been a member of Engineers Without Borders since 2003, and enjoys volunteering for youth programs and conferences about global issues and social change. To decompress, Bev turns to yoga, running, crocheting, or burying her nose in a good book.

Yu-Ling Cheng is the director of the Centre for Global Engineering (CGEN) and professor of chemical engineering and applied chemistry at the University of Toronto. She has a PhD from Stanford University. CGEN was established in 2009 to be the focal point and major driver in preparing engineering graduates for challenges, responsibilities, and opportunities in a globally sustainable future. Under Yu-Ling Cheng's leadership, CGEN is developing new courses and academic programs in global engineering. She also leads several global engineering research initiatives, including a project under the "Re-invent the Toilet" challenge posed by the Bill and Melinda Gates Foundation that has received considerable media attention. She also serves on the board of directors for Academics Without Borders, an NGO whose mission is to enhance higher-education capacity in developing countries. When not working, she golfs, tries to play the piano, and canoes in the Canadian far north.

Donald C. Cole is an associate professor at the University of Toronto and head of the Global Health Division in the Dalla Lana School of Public Health (DLSPH). After a residency at McMaster University, he qualified as a Royal College fellow in occupational medicine (1990) and community medicine (1992). With more than twenty years of health practice, research, and policy work in Canada and in lower- and middle-income countries, he has led multi-stakeholder action research processes in sets of workplaces and communities to change conditions to improve physical and mental health and the economic impacts of such social interventions. He has supervised or co-supervised numerous mixed-methods Masters' and doctoral students, has co-authored over 160 peer-reviewed publications and over 30 chapters, and is the lead editor of a book. During a visiting professorship at Oxford University, he focused on evaluation of graduate programs in global health. He helped develop and became interim director of the Institute for Global Health Equity and Innovation at the University of Toronto.

Carmen Ho is a PhD candidate and SSHRC doctoral fellow in the Department of Political Science at the University of Toronto. She is also manager of the Global Ideas Institute on child malnutrition and co-chair of the university's Interdisciplinary Society for International Development. Her research focuses on sustainable solutions to food insecurity and poverty, and her doctoral work investigates maternal and child nutrition interventions in low- and middle-income countries. Her past experience includes the analysis of nutrition interventions addressing iodine deficiencies with UNICEF and work in the Philippines to scale up sustainable rice production with the Local

Governance Support Program for Local Economic Development (LGSP-LED), a CIDA-funded project. She holds an HBA from the Richard Ivey School of Business at Western University, an MSc in International Public Policy from University College, London (UCL), and has studied at the National University of Singapore.

Anita M. McGahan is associate dean of research, PhD director, professor, and Rotman Chair in Management at the Rotman School of Management at the University of Toronto. She is cross-appointed to the Munk School of Global Affairs; is a senior associate at the Institute for Strategy and Competitiveness at Harvard University; and is chief economist at the Massachusetts General Hospital Division for Global Health and Human Rights. In 2013, she was elected by the Academy of Management's membership to the Board of Governors and into the presidency rotation. Her credits include two books and over 100 articles, case studies, notes, and other published material on competitive advantage, industry evolution, and financial performance. McGahan's current research emphasizes entrepreneurship in the public interest and innovative collaboration between public and private organizations. She is also pursuing a long-standing interest in the inception of new industries, particularly in global health.

Murray R. Metcalfe is Professor, Globalization, with the Centre for Global Engineering in the Faculty of Applied Science and Engineering at the University of Toronto. He holds a BASc in industrial engineering from the University of Toronto and an MS and PhD in engineering-economic systems from Stanford University. He began his professional career at McKinsey and Company, the management consulting firm, and then spent more than twenty years in the venture capital industry in the United States, until returning to academia in 2008. In the spring of 2008 he was a visiting scholar in the Department of International Development Engineering at the Tokyo Institute of Technology. Dr Metcalfe also serves as a senior adviser in the private equity area at an investment management firm in Boston, and is involved in several not-for-profits working in the areas of global development and social entrepreneurship.

Will Mitchell studies business dynamics in developed and emerging markets, investigating how businesses change as their competitive environments change and, in turn, how the business changes contribute to ongoing corporate and social performance. He teaches courses in business dynamics, emerging market strategy, corporate strategy, health sector management, entrepreneurship, and pharmaceutical strategy. Will is the J. Rex Fuqua Professor of International Management at Duke University's Fuqua School of Business. He currently serves as a visiting professor of strategic management in the Rotman School of Management at the University of Toronto, where he holds the Anthony S. Fell Chair in New Technologies and Commercialization. He also has a visiting appointment at the National University of Singapore. Will is a faculty associate of Duke's Global Health Initiative and Center for Entrepreneurship and Innovation, as well as a faculty associate at Rotman's Centre for Health Sector Strategy. Will is a co-editor of the *Strategic Management Journal* and a board member of Neuland Laboratories, Ltd (Hyderabad).

Nandita Perumal is a first-year doctoral student in epidemiology at the University of Toronto with a strong research interest in nutrition implementation and maternal, newborn, and child health in the global context. She received her Master's degree in public health epidemiology, also from the University of Toronto, and holds a BSc in nutritional sciences from McGill University. During her graduate work, Nandita received the Canadian Institutes of Health Research Master's Award and spent time in Kenya working on an agriculture- and health-integrated project to alleviate vitamin A deficiency among pregnant women and their children. Her passion for global health research stems from her experiences of having lived in India, Japan, England, and Canada. She currently works as a global health researcher at the Hospital for Sick Children in Toronto, Canada.

Ashley Aimone Phillips is a Registered Dietitian, specializing in paediatrics, with a Master's degree in nutritional sciences from the University of Toronto. Her general area of academic interest is global child health, with specific interests in micronutrient malnutrition (especially iron-deficiency anaemia) and stunting. Her research efforts are focused on the application of evidence-based practices and research methods to promote the implementation and scale-up of effective interventions for reducing the global burden of child malnutrition and linear growth faltering. She is currently pursuing a doctoral degree in epidemiology (Dalla Lana School of Public Health,

University of Toronto), for which she will use a geographical information system and statistical techniques to develop a model for planning the distribution of micronutrient interventions in low- and middle-income countries. Alongside her doctoral studies, she also holds a part-time research assistantship position with the Sprinkles Global Health Initiative. In her "spare" time, she enjoys spending the short Canadian summers playing golf, sailing, and competing in triathlons.

Rahim Rezaie was a joint research fellow at the Munk School of Global Affairs and the Rotman School of Management (both at the University of Toronto) and is now at the Asia Pacific Foundation of Canada. His research is focused on biotechnology and pharmaceutical innovation in China, India, and Brazil. In this context, he examines the role of indigenous enterprises in these countries in addressing global health needs. He also examines the implications of the rising innovation capacity in the emerging markets for public policy and business strategy in Canada. He has published a series of articles on vaccine, diagnostics, and medicinal innovations by domestic companies in China, India, and Brazil in the *Nature Biotechnology* journal, and elsewhere. His practical experience includes work in genetic testing for a host of hereditary conditions and in pharmaceutical regulatory affairs. Dr Rezaie received a Master's degree in biotechnology and a doctoral degree from the University of Toronto, where he was the recipient of the Banting and Best Canada Graduate Scholarship.

Dilip Soman studies interesting human behaviours and applies his findings to marketing, consumer welfare, and public policy. He has a PhD from the University of Chicago and an MBA from the Indian Institute of Management, and has previously taught at the University of Colorado, the Hong Kong University of Science and Technology (both full time), the Indian School of Business, and the National University of Singapore (as a visiting faculty member). His research in behavioural economics, marketing strategy, social media, CRM/data-driven marketing, pricing, customer engagement, and customer psychology is widely published and cited, and he is a sought-after executive trainer and consultant in these areas. He is also the author of *Managing Customer Value: One Stage at a Time* (World Scientific). His outside interests include photography, watching Bollywood masala movies, and agonizing over successive Indian cricket teams.

Janice Gross Stein is the Belzberg Professor of Conflict Management in the Department of Political Science and the director of the Munk School of Global Affairs at the University of Toronto. She is a Fellow of the Royal Society of Canada and an Honorary Foreign Member of the American Academy of Arts and Sciences. She is the co-author, with Eugene Lang, of the prize-winning *The Unexpected War: Canada in Kandahar*. Her most recent book is *Diplomacy in the Digital Age*. She was the Massey Lecturer in 2001 and a Trudeau Fellow. She was awarded the Molson Prize by the Canada Council for an outstanding contribution by a social scientist to public debate. She has received Honorary Doctorate of Laws degrees from the University of Alberta, the University of Cape Breton, McMaster University, and the Hebrew University of Jerusalem. She is a member of the Order of Canada and the Order of Ontario.

Joseph Wong is the Ralph and Roz Halbert Professor of Innovation at the Munk School of Global Affairs, University of Toronto, professor of political science, and Canada Research Chair in Democratization, Health and Development. He is also the director of the Asian Institute at the Munk School of Global Affairs. In addition to journal articles and contributions to scholarly volumes, Professor Wong's publications include *Healthy Democracies: Welfare Politics in Taiwan and South Korea* (2004) and *Betting on Biotech: Innovation and the Limits of Asia's Developmental State* (2011), both published by Cornell University Press, as well as *Political Transitions in Dominant Party Systems: Learning to Lose*, co-edited with Edward Friedman (2008). Wong has been a visiting scholar at Harvard, Oxford, Seoul National University, National University of Singapore, and the Institute for National Policy Research in Taipei. He has also been an adviser to the United Nations, the World Bank, the Economic Commission for Latin America, and the World Health Organization, as well as for governments in Europe, Africa, Latin America, and Asia.

Stanley Zlotkin is a professor of paediatrics, public health sciences, and nutritional sciences at the Hospital for Sick Children and University of Toronto. He received his MD degree from McMaster University in Hamilton, Ontario, Canada, and his PhD from the University of Toronto. Dr Zlotkin and his program, the Sprinkles Global Health Initiative, have focused on research and advocacy to control malnutrition in children. He is an active researcher, with well over 100 peer-reviewed publications. He was awarded the H.J. Heinz Humanitarian Award in 2001 for his international advocacy work for children globally, the CIHR National Knowledge Translation Award in 2006, and the Order of Canada in 2007, the highest civilian honour in Canada, for his contributions to improving the lives of children globally. Dr Zlotkin was appointed Vice-President, Medical and Academic Affairs, at the Hospital for Sick Children in 2010, and in September 2012 was appointed as the hospital's inaugural chief of Global Child Health.